Getting the Buggers to Read PLAZA

Also available from Continuum:

Other titles in the Buggers series:

Getting the Buggers into Languages – Amanda Barton

Getting the Buggers Fit – Lorraine Cale and Jo Harris

Getting the Buggers to Write 2 – Sue Cowley

Getting the Buggers to Behave 2 – Sue Cowley

Getting the Buggers to Think – Sue Cowley

Letting the Buggers be Creative – Sue Cowley

Getting the Buggers into Science – Christine Farmery

Getting the Buggers to Turn Up – Ian McCormack

Getting the Buggers to Add Up 2 – Mike Ollerton

Getting the Buggers to Draw – Barbara Ward

Other related titles:

Teaching English 3–11 – Cathy Burnett and Julia Myers

Teaching Literacy – Fred Sedgwick

Teaching Poetry – Fred Sedgwick

Getting the Buggers to Read

Claire Senior

continuum

Continuum

The Tower Building   15 East 26th Street
11 York Road   New York
London SE1 7NX   NY 10010

www.continuumbooks.com

British Library Cataloguing-in-Publication Data
A catalogue record for this book is available from the British Library.

ISBN 0–8264–7347–4 (paperback)

Typeset by BookEns Ltd, Royston, Herts.
Printed and bound in Great Britain by
MPG Books Ltd, Bodmin, Cornwall

Contents

Acknowledgements

Thanks to all the students and teachers who talked about books and reading and were so honest with their comments. Thanks also to the schools which have given me the support to try out these ideas and to the writers who allowed me to use their text.

Thanks to Alexandra Webster at Continuum and special thanks to Gerry for tea and constant encouragement.

Introduction

When we think about 'getting the buggers to read' what do we mean? We don't mean that they need to go through the 'reading process' as experts in the teaching of reading say, we mean that we want students to exercise the ability to read that they already have, to choose books as an activity which will figure in their lives and add richness to it. By the time they reach secondary school most of our students will have managed to go through the process and be at least competent readers. They will also have learned a good deal about reading that they have not been taught.

Learning to read is by reading, a truism I know, but worthy of examination because the language element of the texts on which children learn is often ignored. Discussion of the 'process' often implies that the texts are neutral and that we read all texts in the same way. We don't do the same thing with a shopping list, a theatre programme, an email from a friend, yet the difference between the way that we read a web-page and 'no man is an island, entire of itself' is rarely acknowledged. Our students have already learned this as part of their own 'private learning' and when they identify and become emotionally involved with a text they are recognizing those untaught differences.

They have also learned that reading is not necessarily the solitary inward activity that it is seen as. Their involvement with their reading has taught them the pleasures of sharing their responses with others who have enjoyed the same text whether these are parents, teachers, librarians or peers. I hope to suggest activities throughout this book, which take notice of this thinking, which encourages the sharing of responses and acknowledges the 'private learning' that students have already done.

The next question to answer is 'Why do we want to get

students to read?' If you are a parent, it might be because it means you know that reading enriches their lives and helps in their education. It also might help you know exactly where they are and what they are doing. If you're a teacher and you are fully conversant with the National Curriculum and the Literacy Strategy you will know how important it is for them to have 'research and study skills', 'to understand the writer's craft' and 'to explore the notion of literary heritage'; and understanding of 'why some texts have been particularly influential and or significant'. Whichever one of these you are, you might also enjoy books, taking vicarious pleasure in the lives of fictional characters and learning about ideas, emotions and experiences you will not live yourself.

The implementation of the Literacy Strategy has also given students access to a far wider range of texts and the tools to be critical of the material that they read. The questioning of texts in Guided Reading enables students to tackle texts independently and become familiar with ways to access a variety of text types. In this process though, the time for independent reading of personal choice texts has been eroded. When this is relegated to ten minutes at the beginning or end of lessons the message given to students is perhaps not the one we want. It suggests that reading is something easily picked up for a short period and, as we do it regularly, it must be 'good for your health'. It devalues the need for commitment and the focus sometimes necessary to get into a book and may well not be what readers need at the time. If we want to encourage enjoyment wherever it is found and develop enthusiasms for authors, genres or particular books so that our children become readers for life, we need to revisit the place for private reading in the curriculum.

If children are to become lifetime consumers of books then their own reading preferences must be known and accepted and used as the basis for encouragement. They need reader role models, easy access to books in a wide variety of style and genre, and recommendations personally tailored for them.

Paul Jennings famously said: 'There's no such thing as a reluctant reader. There are only readers for whom the right book has not yet been found'. That means that we, as their teachers, need to be very aware of what is available in the world of children's literature so we can help our students become discriminating readers themselves. It means that we have to be able to refute the arguments against the very texts that they enjoy, because they 'aren't good for them'. Comics and graphic novels, for example, because they encourage violence and anti-social behaviour or because they do not reflect the canon, the initial reading list of the National Curriculum. I think we need to celebrate with our students the books that teach alternative ways of looking at the world, and encourage reading that is experimental and occasionally subversive.

When I first began to think about this book, I began to consider why and what I read and to look at my own reading influences to try to see what made me a reader and to contemplate what part reading plays in my own life. If we can do this, ways of encouraging young people to read may become clearer.

I began with thinking about why children should read. So here is my checklist, in no particular order:

- to experience and rehearse situations which they may meet;
- to meet characters and in Atticus Finch's words 'to walk around a while in their shoes';
- to see how the book differs from the film;
- to understand and empathize with emotions and situations not yet met;
- to reach out imaginatively for other worlds;
- to while away travelling time;
- to learn to appreciate the views of others;
- to learn about ideas which will make them think and consider;
- to learn to predict and work out why things happen;
- to practise reading different styles in preparation for moving to adult books;
- to lose yourself;
- to amuse yourself;
- to be able to share enthusiasms with others;
- to learn about what has happened in the world;
- to find out information.

My aim in this book is to try to provide some suggestions to help turn young people into enthusiastic and committed readers or at the very least to provide ideas to encourage reluctant readers to see books as a possible means of enjoyment rather than a chore to be got through. This does mean knowing and endorsing the kind of books young people like to read, keep, and finding ways to encourage them to challenge themselves.

1 The importance of reading

Before launching in to how we encourage students to read I want to look at some books to illustrate what students can learn from them, thus showing some of the reasons why I think reading is so important.

One of the people who had a huge impact on my thinking about reading was Margaret Meek. I was fascinated by *How texts teach what readers learn*, and I regularly think of that when I read a new book to recommend to students. In it she discusses a number of texts which give young people lessons on how to read. She examines how they use the knowledge and experience they already bring to books to interpret the narrative they are dealing with.

She analyses a favourite story of mine, *William's Version* by Jan Mark, which involves a young boy left alone with his grandmother to 'entertain' each other. Gran tries to tell the story of the three little pigs but William constantly diverts the story. It is clear that his mother is having another baby and William regularly refers to that throughout the story as well as all the characters that the third pig kills. Young students listening to this story all identify William's concern for his place in the family with a new brother or sister on the way and even when they are too young to fully articulate it they can understand the sense of displacement that it describes. Narratives are an important link with a reader's unconscious and may reveal to him or her things that they have not formerly recognized.

I want now to look at some books with this knowledge in mind. The first one is Malorie Blackman's *Noughts and Crosses*. For anyone who doesn't know it, it describes a society of segregation between the white Noughts and the black Crosses. Against this background Sephy, a member of the ruling Crosses, and Callum, a poor member of the Nought underclass, fall in love. Malorie Blackman who had been on the receiving end of racism as a young woman growing up in Britain was determined to avoid showing black people as victims as many stories about black people do and this was the genesis of this book. The young people who read it are gripped by it and for many it is the first time that they recognize some of the prejudices inherent in society. There is one simple scene where a Nought needs attention for an injury and comments on how strange the brown plaster looks on white skin. Students pick up on this and are often horrified by it. For many this simple comment brings home the significance of being a minority group whose existence is barely recognized especially in the everyday ways that we live our lives.

The book also describes the roots of terrorism and although it does not come down on the side of the terrorists it does show some sympathy for those who have no other way to make their feelings known. The Romeo and Juliet quality of the story of the young lovers captures the emotions of young people who empathize with Sephy and Callum. The novel also disturbs them because they are confronted with feelings about a prejudice that either they did not know existed or considered to be irrelevant to their lives.

Although not all teenage novels do deal so directly with contentious issues a quick trawl through some of the most popular novelists for young people does reveal a number who identify the importance of tapping in to the unconscious concerns of their audience. Adele Geras does just this in *Watching the Roses* which plays with the story of Sleeping Beauty. She often uses young girls' knowledge of fairy tales like this to explore sensitive issues about young adulthood. A girl is raped at her eighteenth birthday party and takes to her bed refusing to speak or engage with the outside world. Her eighteenth birthday signalled her move into womanhood and its attendant sexuality but the rape makes her try to deny this. She wants to become a medieval stone princess with no emotions and barely eats enough to stay alive. The story deals with the classic after-effects of rape, and also of anorexia, of guilt and violation.

It is clear from these texts that literature for young people has changed, from the conservative canon listed by the National

Curriculum, to texts that challenge the portrayal of childhood as a safe place where even difficult situations (Dad in prison, single-parent family living in poverty ... *The Railway Children*) have happy endings. There are books that will disturb young people with the sense of the underlying threat of the ordinary (Neil Gaiman's *Coraline*, with the ever-smiling mum with the button eyes, who won't let her free until she has solved the riddle), and stories which accept that there is nightmare in even the most everyday actions like playing computer games (Alan Gibbons's *The Shadow of the Minotaur*). Although in both these stories there is a resolution at the end, each child suffers to free the parents; the protective parental role is reversed and the child has to learn to draw on his/her own skills to control their lives.

Rather than retreating to a never-never land which reflects the fantasy world of dreams, today's literature teaches young people how powerful words are in constructing a view of the world. They are introduced to ideas which in their context become natural. *Noughts and Crosses* passes on a strong belief that racism is wrong and encourages the reader to resist the ideology that is demonstrated in the text. The reader challenges the assumptions that are made in the text through identification with Callum and Sephy. This ability to identify the cultural position of a text is an essential part of critical literacy.

As well as entertainment, literature for young people also helps to prepare them for the range of fiction that they will meet as adults. Literature has long established the idea of drawing attention to a text as constructed and fictional. Characters draw attention to their own fictional nature, 'Reader, I married him', to re-order narrative and comment on it, all ways of rejecting any attempt by the reader to lose themselves in the book. John Fowles's *The French Lieutenant's Woman* takes this to the extreme by providing readers with two endings from which they choose their preference. Children's texts also like to play with this idea. In Cornelia Funke's *Inkheart* the characters from stories are 'read' into existence by the power of the reader's voice. When they meet their creator they deny his existence and quarrel with his right to determine what happens to them. Accepting metafiction at this level prepares them for later readings of books like *Tristram Shandy* and *The French Lieutenant's Woman*.

It is vital that, as teachers, we have knowledge of these texts and the ways in which they work, to know what we are presenting to young people and to encourage their development as readers by offering texts which will speak to them about their lives and their fears, and will help to develop their understanding of the world. We often choose literature which reflects our view of the world and reinforces it, but often it can take us on journeys which we hadn't expected and the more widely we expose children to these 'roads not taken' the more we teach them about what it means to be human.

Reluctant readers

For many of us the pleasure to be gained from a good book is enough to keep us reading. In *Inkheart* by Cornelia Funke, Meggie tells of the way that pages whisper to her of the tales inside, and how if the story is an old favourite the whispering is different from that of a new tale to be discovered. Our reluctant readers don't hear that whispering or can easily ignore it.

Reluctant readers come in a number of guises: they include the intelligent children who are interested in reading but who don't read well; those who seem to have little or no interest and who, because they read so rarely, are in danger of falling behind their peers; and those children who have specific problems that make reading difficult. The most frustrating one is the reader who reads well but chooses not to.

These all provide different problems for the English teacher. Those with specific problems can be addressed with the Special Needs department who will provide reading support for them and help to try to bring their reading ages up to that of their peers. With all the others, finding the right material can be the biggest spur to encouraging them to accept and embrace reading but this is not always easy with students who say that they never read and prefer to play sport, hang around with their friends, watch television, play computer games, in fact anything but read. It is interesting that NFER research shows that the drive to improve standards of literacy through the introduction of the Literacy Strategy has succeeded in making more confident and independent readers, but during the same period, 1998–2003, Marian

Sainsbury, chief researcher, found that reading for pleasure has declined. Of course this may be only a reflection of the changes in society during that period.

Faced with this decline in interest we need to determine what student interests are and try to use these to encourage reading. Throughout this book there are suggestions to help you to attract reluctant readers. If the purpose of encouraging reading is twofold:

- to gain enjoyment and pleasure from texts;
- to improve literacy;

then it follows that they need to be reading anything which sparks interest even if it doesn't always fulfil the English teacher's desire for them to enjoy fiction. A number of suggestions for areas of interest are explored in the 'suggestions for books' boxes: sport-related material, e.g. non-fiction books related to skateboarding, mountain biking, extreme sports; a counter for those who 'don't see any point in reading about made-up things'; in true-life stories and anything that deals with the tallest, largest, longest or nastiest. The links to computer games will be further explored as a source of reading material and there will be suggestions for getting them to read 'by the back door'.

Part One

Whole School

2 Reading autobiography

One of the concerns shared by parents and teachers alike is that reading is declining as a leisure activity among teenagers, particularly boys. This is borne out by the results of surveys like that carried out by the Schools Health Education Unit based at Exeter University which showed a drop in the numbers of teenagers who read for pleasure. In 1991 25 per cent of 14- and 15-year-old boys said that they would choose to read in their spare time, whereas by 1998 that figure had dropped to 18 per cent. Research has also been done in Scotland whose findings also suggest a sharp decline in reading, with sport, playing computer games and watching television all taking a much higher profile. Many of the suggestions in this book are here to help you to find ways to encourage these reluctant readers to participate. Although these research results may all sound very bleak, the picture is not all bad and is different across the range of schools. Carrying out a reading audit in your school, in one year group, or at least among your own classes will help you to gain a perspective on the situation.

First, it sounds obvious, but you need to know exactly what you want to find out before you devise your questions. The questions below suggest areas that might be interesting to follow up and might work well for one class but would generate a great deal of data if they were spread to a large year group.

- How many boys/girls in Year 7 choose to read for pleasure?
- Is this different in other year groups?
- Is this any different from a year ago?
- Where do they choose to read?
- Who influences their choice of books?
- What genres do they read in?

- What do they read apart from fiction?
- Does television or film influence their reading?

If you only want to audit your own classes, I find that asking them to create their own reading autobiography is more useful to me. It allows me to find out how they see themselves as readers and to find out where they are currently. I allow a lesson or maybe two and a homework for this, near the beginning of term when we are beginning to get to know each other. We begin by reminiscing about their earliest memories of books. Once some begin to name names they spur each other on and dredge up books they have completely forgotten. Some can still recite the texts of particular favourites and many still have them in their rooms. We discuss who read to them and their favourite places with their reasons why. Many remember books which scared them and which they could only listen to from the safety of a lap. They then write the first section on their earliest memories. We also talk about earliest toys and for students who cannot remember being read to I ask them to write about the earliest games they can remember playing or their earliest toys.

The next section is about learning to read and once they are in the reflective mode they usually have some lovely and, over the years, some horrible stories. One student used to cheat at the reading-scheme books to try to get on to the stories with the covers that he really liked the look of. My own son used to read his school reading book to our cat saying that she'd enjoy it more than he did. Students talk about being competitive, reading that they found easy and difficult, books and authors they most enjoyed and how they were helped to overcome obstacles. As the discussion can take some time they often finish writing this up as homework.

Then I ask them to think about becoming independent readers and the end of primary school: authors they liked reading; books that made a particular impression on them; any genre awareness and who influenced them. They write too about how much they used to read in Year 6, what their favourite places for reading were and whether they still liked being read to.

The final section is about how they see themselves as readers now. Have their reading habits changed? Do they still read as much, and why or why not? Has their taste in reading changed? Are they still influenced by the same people? Do they have a favourite author or genre? Are there again any books that they know that they want to read but haven't yet?

As I said earlier just taking part in the exercise helps to raise the status of reading in the classroom. Many students bring in old favourite books and these are enjoyed again and some students begin to discuss books with others which stimulates book sharing. When we discuss the final section many of the books they talk about are in the room so it is also an opportunity to provide them for borrowing.

Activities such as this, which focus students' attention on themselves as readers and which remind many of them of their enjoyment of reading, can be a stimulus to reacquainting themselves with the pleasure of books. This can expand across the whole school when a reading audit is carried out as it may raise the profile of reading for your students.

Having established the significance of reading in students' lives I want to identify and examine some of the ways in which we can present them with texts which will help to bring about some of the features that I described earlier. Some of these deal with the way in which a whole-school programme can influence the view of reading, others look at the ways in which individual teachers can present reading as an attractive proposition. Some of these ideas are more appropriate to Key Stage 3 but there are activities which can work equally well with older students and there are suggestions for helping A-level students to read around set texts and to broaden the scope of their reading. Finally I want to address some of the issues around the various sorts of reluctant readers and suggest some ways of helping to tackle their problems.

The first area to look at is to create a school in which reading is seen to be valued.

3 Creating a reader-friendly school

The Literacy Trust reported on research which foregrounds the importance of reading. It suggests that, 'Enthusiasm about reading a range of diverse material is a more important factor in success in literacy at age 15 than having well-educated parents in good jobs'. Willingness to tackle texts which challenge them gives students access to a greater diversity of information, more open minds and a wider choice of material to draw on.

This obviously has implications for how we encourage students to be readers by choice. Schools need to show to all those who enter that it is a place which values reading and welcomes readers in all shapes or forms as in individual English classrooms. It is a good exercise for you to carry out an audit on your school. Spend some time walking around the buildings and try to look at them with the eyes of parents visiting with a new student. What message would they get from that tour? Start with the entrance to the school and visit all the areas including those not obviously associated with literacy. Here is a list of areas to look at with some suggestions for showing that your school takes literacy seriously:

- Reception: this is often a place where visitors wait, so it is a good place to showcase some of the activities that you do as a school. These can be photographs of specific reading events or of staff and students reading, recommended reads by students, graphs/charts of favourite books, a book of reviews by students and advertisements for specific events such as book fairs which may be coming up. It is good if the photographs show a diversity of material being read, e.g. newspapers and comics, picture books and graphic novels and fiction and non-fiction.

- Corridors or any open areas in the school: any display space could carry some of the above as well as posters advertising particular authors and books, both commercial posters and ones created by students. It is good if this is true throughout the school not just in the area where the English Department live. We created posters one year on which we mounted reviews of books which staff had read over the summer holidays. These reviews could be changed at regular intervals with other staff and students reviews. It is useful to recruit all staff who work in a school to write reviews for you. This should include the caretaking staff, the dinner ladies, the lunchtime staff and any of the office workers.

To ensure that the varying tastes of staff are represented, a team of interested volunteers could carry out brief interviews and write up the reviews for them. It is important that a real cross-section of material is represented here. I always read, with awe, the lists of esoteric books that celebrities are going to take on holiday with them. For many of them I would need access to my dictionary and a selection of reference books. Those questioned often say that they have little time for reading and catch up during their holidays. Many of the tomes mentioned would certainly help me to catch up – on my sleep! We need to ensure that my sense of alienation does not apply around the school. If students only see adults reading things that would seem to be a) beyond their ability and b) totally out of their interest, then we are losing the chance to use adults as models of reading practice for them. Reading needs to be seen as entertainment and enjoyment for ordinary people. For this reason it is useful to try to involve as many departments as possible in demonstrating an enthusiasm for reading.

Some are very easy, e.g. history, where a list of novels linked to the areas of the curriculum could be displayed, or geography, where stories which give a vivid evocation of another part of the world could be on hand. A list of scientists who are also writers would make a good poster as well as copies of the 'Horrible' series. It doesn't matter if the links are quite tenuous, e.g. *The Curious Incident of the Dog in the Night-time* linked to prime numbers might work well in mathematics! Book reviews by students on subject-specific books could be used for display as well as posters created by students to introduce authors who are particularly related to a subject area. A walk around the science block can provide plenty of opportunities for recognizing literacy. Many departments have a variety of posters on display which introduce students to scientists or specific discoveries. Posters advertising the Horrible Science range of books are colourful and the books, like the historical ones, often collect together the most gruesome bits of information which youngsters get a great deal of pleasure from. There are also fiction texts, particularly in the genre of science fiction, which can introduce scientific subjects in a challenging and enjoyable way. The genre is enormous and it is hard to know where to start, but there are some classics which posit situations which are a direct result of scientific discovery or development which a science department might use or at least have available for students.

There will be a wide selection of book titles in the Appendix but I want to include some suggestions which link in to the specific subjects under discussion as we go along.

Texts linked to history

Key Stage 3

The Midwife's Apprentice	Karen Cushman	Medieval life
Coram Boy	Jamila Gavin	18th century
Ruby in the Smoke	Philip Pullman	19th century
War Horse	Michael Morpurgo	WWI
Private Peaceful	Michael Morpurgo	
Friedrich	Hans Peter Richter	WWII
I am David	Anne Holm	
Carrie's War	Nina Bawden	
Kensuke's Kingdom	Michael Morpurgo	
Goodnight Mister Tom	Michael Magorian	

Key Stage 4

Across the Barricades	Joan Lingard	Northern Ireland
Final Journey	Gudrun Pausewang	Holocaust
When the Wind Blows	Raymond Biggs	WWII

Heroes	Robert Cormier	WWII
The Shell House	Linda Newbury	WWI
Some Other War	Linda Newbury	
Remembrance	Theresa Breslin	
The Sterkarm Handshake	Susan Price	Time travel

Books with a strong evocation of place

Key Stage 3

The Garbage King	Elizabeth Laird	Ethiopia
A Journey to the River Sea	Eva Ibbotson	South America
The Thief Lord	Cornelia Funke	Venice
Kensuke's Kingdom	Michael Morpurgo	Desert island in the Pacific ocean
Plundering Paradise	Geraldine McCaughrean	Madagascar
Gulf	Robert Westall	Set in the Gulf War

Key Stage 4

No 1 Ladies' Detective Agency	James Alexander McCall Smith	Africa
Roll of Thunder Hear My Cry	Mildred Taylor	Southern states of America ... good too for history of racism in America
Talking in Whispers	James Watson	Chile in Pinochet's time
Hideous Kinky	Esther Freud	Morocco
Skindeep	Toecky Jones	South Africa
The Frozen Waterfall	Gaye Hicyilmaz	This begins in Turkey then moves to Switzerland. It makes interesting contrasts between them
Bury the Dead	Peter Carter	Berlin before the wall came down

Books and science

Key Stage 3

Z for Zachariah	Robert O'Brien
When the Wind Blows	Raymond Briggs
Plague 99	Jean Ure
Silent Spring	Rachel Carson (this is old but still great)
The Giver	Lois Lowry
Eva	Peter Dickenson
Mrs Frisby and the Rats of Nimh	Robert O'Brien
Mortal Engines	Philip Reeve
Empty World	John Christopher

Key Stage 4

Frankenstein	Mary Shelley
Journey to the Centre of the Earth	Jules Verne
The Foundation Series	Isaac Asimov
Brother in the Land	Robert Swindells
A Bone from the Sea	Peter Dickinson
The Death of Grass	John Christopher
The Plague Dogs	Richard Adams

Computers and work in ICT provides a rich source of opportunities for encouraging reading and there will be a whole section devoted to this a little later. There are, however, some ways in which you can tap in to the facilities to indicate and encourage the school's enthusiasm for reading.

- If you have a school Intranet this is a good place for book recommendations. We have an entry page which is separated into Key Stages and then further into subjects. This entry page could include a booklist of suggestions for that Key Stage with reviews from students. Quirky lines from these reviews can then be used to make up posters in the Library to entice students to read the whole review.

- If you have email facility in school then students could email their friends with the titles of anything that they have enjoyed reading recently. Many teachers also have friends who teach in other schools and reading discussions and exchange of book recommendations can be set up using the Internet. For those of you who are devotees of the Teachit website (www.teachit.co.uk) you could use the staffroom section to contact other schools to find someone who might have students who would be interested in exchanging suggestions for reading. The staffroom notice board is used by teachers in Australia too so it could be an interesting exchange.

Another source for the development of ideas to create a reader-friendly school is the National Literacy Trust. It was set up in 1993 and is 'an independent charity dedicated to building a literate nation'. Their aim is to raise 'literacy standards for all age groups throughout the UK'. Their website, www.literacytrust.org.uk/index.html is an invaluable resource for teachers, with very good links to websites which are user-friendly both for teachers and students. If you go to the website:

- you can use the menu on the left, under NLT Initiatives, to reach Reading Connects;
- use the menu on the left to go to 'practical ideas';
- click on 'making reading visible'.

I particularly liked the idea of their Real Men Read campaign which aims to provide male role models in schools. These are male staff, students or members of the local community who are pictured reading, often with books which have a specific appeal to men. The Reading Champions model is also a good idea here. Staff, parents and students (older boys can be good role models) could be recorded talking about their favourite reading and these interviews could be accessed from the Intranet.

Another idea which I particularly like is to set up a reading list for 'stressed teachers'. A group of students could collect from staff a list of their favourite holiday reading, or staff could send it back to school on a postcard from wherever they are on holiday. These could then be displayed somewhere prominent in school. The

World Book Day activity for 2005 also built on this idea, by producing postcards which people could send to anyone they knew with a recommended read on them. They were asked to suggest a title and give a reason why they thought the recipient would enjoy it or, in some cases, should read it. Students and staff could copy this idea by sending postcards to friends via a school mailbox.

Your initial walk around the school to assess the message given about the value put on literacy may well have shown you a great deal more going on than you thought. Whether it did or didn't, it is useful to enlist the support of interested members of a number of the departments and try to start in a small way to demonstrate their support for literacy.

4 Events

In this chapter I am going to look at how reading can be made a special event in school. This means acknowledging that reading, as well as being something that some children do as often and as naturally as breathing, can also be given a much higher profile and be seen by a wider spectrum of people. The fevered excitement surrounding the publication of *Harry Potter and the Half-Blood Prince* demonstrated the importance of reading in the lives of a significant number of young people (and their parents).

For many children it is important to have their passion taken as seriously as is their contemporaries' passion for football. Events in school, whether as large as a whole-school Reading Festival which I will deal with separately as it can be a big event, or as small as a reading group, can legitimize their interest and can encourage others to take part.

Shadowing the Carnegie Award

This is a lovely exercise to take part in particularly as it takes place at the tail end of the school year in June/July when enthusiasms have a tendency to wane. Every year the Chartered Institute of Library and Information Professionals (CILIP) award The Carnegie Medal to the writer of an outstanding book for children. The award was originally established in 1936 to honour the memory of the Scottish-born philanthropist Andrew Carnegie who used the fortune that he made in the steel industry in America to set up more than 2,800 libraries across the English-speaking world. Its first winner was Arthur Ransome's *Pigeon Post*. The winners since then still read like a list of teacher suggestions for good reading for teenagers but are also a fruitful area for discussion with young people. How many of these books are still popular and read today? How many of the most recent winners do they think will still be read in 70 years' time?

Full list of winners

Please note that the year refers to when the book was published rather than when the medal was awarded, i.e. the 2001 winner was announced and the medal presented in July 2002.

2003 Jennifer Donnelly	*A Gathering Light*	Bloomsbury
2003 Sharon Creech	*Ruby Holler*	Bloomsbury
2002 Terry Pratchett	*The Amazing Maurice and his Educated Rodents*	Doubleday
2000 Beverley Naidoo	*The Other Side of Truth*	Puffin
1999 Aidan Chambers	*Postcards from No Man's Land*	Bodley Head
1998 David Almond	*Skellig*	Hodder Children's Books
1997 Tim Bowler	*River Boy*	OUP
1996 Melvin Burgess	*Junk*	Andersen Press
1995 Philip Pullman	*His Dark Materials Book 1 Northern Lights*	Scholastic
1994 Theresa Breslin	*Whispers in the Graveyard*	Methuen
1993 Robert Swindells	*Stone Cold*	Hamish Hamilton
1992 Anne Fine	*Flour Babies*	Hamish Hamilton
1991 Berlie Doherty	*Dear Nobody*	Hamish Hamilton
1990 Gillian Cross	*Wolf*	OUP
1989 Anne Fine	*Goggle-eyes*	Hamish Hamilton
1988 Geraldine McCaughrean	*A Pack of Lies*	OUP
1987 Susan Price	*The Ghost Drum*	Faber
1986 Berlie Doherty	*Granny was a Buffer Girl*	Methuen
1985 Kevin Crossley-Holland	*Storm*	Heinemann
1984 Margaret Mahy	*The Changeover*	Dent
1983 Jan Mark	*Handles*	Kestrel
1982 Margaret Mahy	*The Haunting*	Dent
1981 Robert Westall	*The Scarecrows*	Chatto & Windus
1980 Peter Dickinson	*City of Gold*	Gollancz

1979 Peter Dickinson	*Tulku*	Gollancz
1978 David Rees	*The Exeter Blitz*	Hamish Hamilton
1977 Gene Kemp	*The Turbulent Term of Tyke Tiler*	Faber
1976 Jan Mark	*Thunder and Lightnings*	Kestrel
1975 Robert Westall	*The Machine Gunners*	Macmillan
1974 Mollie Hunter	*The Stronghold*	Hamish Hamilton
1973 Penelope Lively	*The Ghost of Thomas Kempe*	Heinemann
1972 Richard Adams	*Watership Down*	Rex Collings
1971 Ivan Southall	*Josh*	Angus & Robertson
1970 Leon Garfield & Edward Blishen	*The God Beneath the Sea*	Longman
1969 Kathleen Peyton	*The Edge of the Cloud*	OUP
1968 Rosemary Harris	*The Moon in the Cloud*	Faber
1967 Alan Garner	*The Owl Service*	Collins
1966 prize withheld as no book considered suitable		

Many schools take part in a shadowing exercise which begins when the short list is announced in late April/early May each year and continues until the awards ceremony in July. The short list is often eagerly awaited by students who have taken part the previous year or who have been alerted to it by their teachers. The long list is published in March and spotting the ones which will make it to the short list is a good game. The short list can be a very fruitful area for discussion, developing the critical faculties of the young people involved. Why have these particular books been chosen? Why have particular authors or books that the students have recently read been left out? Look at the long list for the year which is usually published earlier in the year. Do the titles/authors on this list differ from those for other major book awards like the *Guardian* Children's fiction prize or the Whitbread Literary Award children's list?

This activity is often run jointly by interested members of English departments and the school library or resource centre. The student group seems usually to be Lower School but some schools use it successfully with Key Stage 4 students, particularly as some of the titles are often from the young adult categories. We open the group to any students in Years 7, 8 and 9, and English teachers encourage students that they know to be keen readers to join in. If you use the county library service they will often provide multiple copies of the books, but if you have to buy them it is possible to get them discounted from Peters Bookselling Services, supporters of the scheme, if you pre-order before the short list is announced. We use these afterwards in book boxes with copies of the reviews written by the students for each classroom. Numbers of students in the groups do vary with some going to meetings every week without fail and others popping in just to get the next book.

There are usually six or seven books on the list and they vary from those intended for young teenagers to those aimed at the 14-plus age group. This can cause a few complications as the content of books in the latter group may not be suitable for younger students. This has been true of a number of the winners in recent years, for example *Junk* by Melvin Burgess, winner in 1996, *Postcards from No Man's Land* by Aidan Chambers, 1999's winner, *The Shell House* by Linda Newbury and *Across the Nightingale Floor* by Lian Hearn. The issue of censorship is a tricky one and, while we probably wouldn't want to censor what students read, parents may need to be involved in making decisions about whether or not their children read these books. I get round this by writing to parents detailing the content of the book and why they may feel it is inappropriate. We then offer them the chance of reading the books first if they would like to. No one yet has ever refused and many of the students say that their parents read the books and they discuss the issues that might be controversial with them.

This aspect of reading as a device for opening up sensitive debates is, I think, a very important one. It allows discussion of situations, like that of homosexuality in *The Shell House*, which often don't otherwise get an airing in an open discussion. This is especially important for boys as it gives them a legitimate reason to be having this discussion without the suspicion of a personal involvement. My students, both boys and girls, were very sympathetic to the difficulties that one of the central characters found himself in when he was attracted to another boy.

During our initial meeting to select the first books to read, the students are given the criteria that the judges use to select the winner. This ensures that the reading becomes purposeful and means that they have to exercise their critical skills throughout. After that we meet once a week. Some students come along only to have a quiet place to continue their books while others are ready to talk. Those who have completed their books make up groups with others who have read the same book. They use the criteria to discuss their book. These groups are usually cross-gender and cross-age. Through this system students develop their understanding of the value of their own opinion, realizing that their choices may not be the same as their peers'. The criteria can be found on the Carnegie Award website: www.carnegiegreenaway.org.uk. This is a very valuable resource as it includes a blurb of each of the books with pictures of the front covers and author profiles and more importantly has access to the Postroom.

The Postroom is where students can write and post their own reviews of the books that they have read as well as read the reviews of students in other schools who are taking part in the scheme. To use this you need to register your school's interest. You will be given a password to access the website and you will need to read and OK the reviews by your students before they can be posted. The involvement in the Shadowing scheme has grown tremendously and the list of schools taking part now runs into hundreds. In fact, in 2004 there were 15,974 reviews posted!

As teachers, the benefits of a scheme such as this are very clear: students who read widely have their reading validated; it creates networks of readers within a school which may continue after the scheme is over; the opportunity to discuss texts with other readers; and reading as an activity is given validity. If you discuss the scheme with students they recognize many of the same benefits as we do and pleasingly arrive at similar judgements quite independently. Added benefits can also be found in their own judgements. Reading is often seen as a solitary activity and there are parents who encourage their children to be out 'doing' something rather than reading. Many of my students joined the Carnegie shadowing because 'all my friends go' and enjoy the opportunity to 'compare lots of different ideas with other people'. Many of them relished the chance to 'discuss what you like and dislike about the books'. So many of them mentioned this that it reinforced for me the reason for the still growing success of reading groups for adults. Although the discussion groups used the judges' criteria their discussions ranged much more widely, particularly when there was dissent. Some students noted this, citing greater confidence gained through discussion, particularly with other students. One particularly perceptive student recognized that writing even a negative review of the book was interesting because it helped to formulate her opinions while the lure of words in print on a website was clearly very strong.

Many schools record the participation in the group with a certificate and we hold a mini-celebration at the final meeting before voting. This meeting usually takes place on the day before the winner is announced. We usually have a loud and vociferous argument about our winning choice. 2004 was sharply divided between the older students who voted for the Young Adult choices and the younger students who were happier with the 11–14 selection. Rarely do all the students agree on a clear winner so we vote and post our results on our Carnegie display board. I put up the judges' result as soon as I can and it's great to see the number of students who visit the board and to hear the discussions which take place around it. The announcement does sometimes come as a bit of an anti-climax, particularly if something is chosen which none of the students wanted. We can also send in our school vote to the website where the results of the student poll are displayed for comparison with the librarians' vote.

It could be argued that schemes like this do little to develop readers, only reinforce the skills of already good readers who will read alone regularly regardless of such interventions. I would defend it from the point of view of students who can be marginalized for their 'bookishness'. This legitimizes their enthusiasm, often providing a development of critical faculties for the gifted and talented in school. Finally, it does not only appeal to the 'good readers'. One year we had a student who struggled with reading, who could not have completed any of the novels on the list without a great deal of support. He happened on the Greenaway texts which had been sent to us by mistake so embarked on a reading of all of them. It included Anthony Browne's *Voices in the Park* and he gave a very sophisticated reading of the symbols in the pictures to all of the students involved in the scheme. The area of the Greenaway Award is one that could be developed to allow access to the Shadowing scheme for a wider number of students.

5 Reading Festivals

A whole-school Reading Festival is one of the biggest events to describe. It celebrates reading for all students regardless of age or ability. World Book Day, in which all students are given book vouchers for £1, can be a good time to hold a Reading Festival. This can be as big or small as you have time and resources for. It has perhaps become more important as a way to promote reading of whole books rather than textual extracts, and meeting and working with favourite authors is an experience which many students cherish.

Inviting authors

If you are planning a Reading Festival you need to start planning about a year ahead, particularly if you would like to invite popular authors as many of them are very busy. It is good to enlist the help of enthusiastic colleagues and a small group is very useful for sharing out the jobs. A first meeting would make decisions on the possible activities and finalize which ones would work in your school. Here are some possibilities but I am sure that you could think of many more.

Reading Festival activities

- Invite author/s
- Preparation for visit/day of visit
- Competitions
- Theme
- Sponsorship
- Timetables

- Staff/student involvement
- Bookfair
- Cross-curricular activities

There are two things to decide before anything else: if you want to have a theme and which authors you are going to try for. Decide on at least four if you can so that you have fall-back positions if the first ones cannot come. If you are flexible about dates it will obviously be easier. Many schools want to build a Reading Festival around National Book Week; if you do this you need to make your first contacts with your chosen authors at least a year in advance. Another possible way is to use Book Week as a time to prepare students for an author visit around your own Festival at a later date.

If you are going to work on a fairly small scale, choosing a theme based around either students' current interests or a particularly popular book might be a good idea. Of course this may again limit your choice of authors.

Choosing authors is an interesting exercise. Try to involve a number of people in the decision-making so that many possibilities can be suggested. While popular authors are obviously very good, talking with colleagues in other schools can be useful in trying to find less popular writers who have been good with students. Writers who are less well known are often very keen to come into schools to talk to students and it can be helpful to both sides. It is also often less expensive than inviting the top children's authors. Your budget needs to cover their fee, their travel expenses and, if they are travelling a long way, overnight expenses, although some may be prepared to stay with staff. If you have to cover both travel and overnight stay, it is worth contacting other local schools and see if they may wish to use the writer for a second day and split costs with you.

There are some very helpful websites when you are looking for possible writers. Jubilee Books has a comprehensive site which lists authors, gives advice and offers Bookfairs.

Jubilee Books
Eltham Green School Complex
Middle Park Avenue
London SE9 5EQ
Tel   020 8850 7676   (9.30–5.30)
Fax   020 8294 0345
email Jubilee Books
www.jubileebooks.co.uk

Another very useful website is the Book Trust which gives you access to a database of artists who are prepared to work with people of all ages. It includes the fields of music, art and literature and gives you all the information you need to contact writers. The third website in the following box is that of the National Centre for Language and Literacy. This is a very useful website as it too has a large database of authors as well as a collection of resources, a list of their publications and various courses and conferences which they run. You can search the database by area of the country, skill (i.e. poetry, drama, illustrator, novelist) and age range and full details of how to contact the author, i.e. through their publisher, at their home address or by telephone or email.

www.booktrusted.co.uk/cbw/visit.html
www.nawe.co.uk
www.ncll.reading.ac.uk

Preparation for day of visit/day of visit

Once an author has agreed to come it is important to confirm all the details. A letter should include:

- the date and time;
- your school's name and address (details of how to get there and arrangements for meeting them depending on their form of transport);
- length and number of sessions;
- fee and expenses to be paid;

- method of payment. (I have always found that they prefer to be paid on the day, so it's useful to let them know if you will need an invoice. If payment on the day is not possible then it should always be made promptly, because writers have to cover their own costs.)

It is also important to make sure that each of you knows what is expected. Some writers are happy to work with large groups; one very memorable occasion for our school was a visit from performance poet Andrew Fusek Peters. He said that he was quite happy to have the whole of Year 9 (about 300) students. We were rather sceptical about this and arranged quite a high staff/student ratio but within a very short time he held the entire hall in his hand. He could have managed without any staff there except perhaps to hold back the deluge of students to buy his books and get them signed at the end of the session. Other writers prefer to work with small groups and again a very memorable visit was that of Philippa Pearce who was nearly 80 at the time. We selected students carefully, only sending those who had read her books and who were excited to meet her. Of course one aspect of organizing events like this means that you too get to meet favourite authors and I had known and enjoyed her books since reading *Tom's Midnight Garden* as a child, so I too was a little in awe of meeting her.

A number of writers prefer to talk about their own writing and particularly a current book and will give insights into how they work, answering questions from students who always want to know the genesis of particular ideas or characters. They are particularly interested in whether writers use any details or situations that they discover from the students that they meet on school visits. One student asked which children's book the writer would like to have written and why, which opened a wide discussion between the author and students on their favourite reading.

Another possibility is to use writers who would be happy to run creative writing workshops. These will often mean smaller groups but can be very rewarding both for you and your students. This always has a tremendous spin-off in their writing, although it may not be noticed until some time later. It also allows for individual work on issues like the benefits of first- and third-person writing and discussion on the pros and cons of plot planning. Philip Pulman's rather subversive advice to students faced with Key Stage tests is to write the story first, then the plan.

You should also clarify with the author if he/she wants you to arrange for the local bookseller to provide books or if they will bring them. You should also ensure that the students are well prepared and know that they may need to bring money if they wish to buy copies of the books the author has talked about. Copies which are personally signed for them often become treasured possessions. It is also useful to clarify beforehand if any special equipment, e.g. overhead projectors or flip charts, will be needed.

While you will want to make the most of the visit, remember that it is tiring for your visitor, so do not timetable the whole day for them. Make arrangements with them to ensure that they are comfortable with the timetable you have prepared and make sure that students are well prepared for the visit having read or studied a selection of books by the author. It is a good idea to use prior lessons to ensure that they have a variety of questions to ask. This not only makes the session more stimulating for them; it also ensures a contented author at the end of the session.

Finally, a visiting author once told me of a school she visited where at lunchtime she was left to her own devices, not offered lunch or even a drink during the day. Both would seem to me to be necessities. School lunches may not be wonderful but often writers like the opportunity that eating in the canteen gives to watch and talk to children and staff.

Competitions

If you are holding a Reading Festival lasting a week or more it is often a good idea to include a number of competitions which relate to books. Many primary schools have a 'Dress up as your favourite character' day, however, discussion with secondary students, even Year 7, suggests that they feel themselves too sophisticated for that. Visual representations of scenes in film posters, bookmarks and posters advertising the coming festival always seem to be more appropriate. This is usually a good way to create a more cross–curricular event. The art department is often keen to be involved; some staff will help students plan entries and someone will always judge them for you. It is possible to help provide funds for prizes by laminating the prizewinning bookmarks and selling them.

The above are voluntary entries but you may also choose to have competitions which all students take part in, run through the English department. These can include creative writing on the festival theme if you have one, or on subjects chosen by the students. These can then be judged by a group of students perhaps from another year group.

Theme

When you have booked your author/authors you may wish to try to focus on a particular theme if there is a link between them or if you have one author visiting who writes in one particular genre. Building on the success of Harry Potter could create a focus on books involving magic and introducing students to a wider range of writers whose work they might enjoy.

The Wizard of Earthsea	Ursula Le Guin
Fire and Hemlock	Diana Wynn Jones
The Book of Dead Days	Martin Sedgewick
His Dark Materials	Philip Pullman
Witch Child	Celia Rees
Sabriel	Garth Nix
The Changeover	Margaret Mahy
The Ghost Drum	Susan Cooper
Circle of Magic	Tamora Pierce
The Hounds of the Morrigan	Pat O'Shea

Books involving magic are obviously closely linked to fantasy, so any booklist which suggests one will include the other. There are a number of good websites which will help you to find books on any particular subject. www.seemore.mi.org/booklists/ is particularly good as you can choose particular subjects, age groups or suggestions of linked books. They are compiled by librarians so have a great deal of currency in knowing what young people read.

Sponsorship

Funding for a Reading Festival can be organized in a number of ways. If you are working on a fairly small scale it may be possible to fund it out of departmental capitation, perhaps in conjunction with the school library or resource centre. Some projects, such as competition prizes, can be funded from the sale of such things as laminated bookmarks (see section above on Competitions). Local businesses may also support reading initiatives in school. We once had a literary quiz with questions in shops in the High Street. Each participating shop had a question on popular fiction, mostly children's, prominently displayed in the window and students had a list of shops to find the questions. The shops also had the books which were to be given as prizes for the winners.

Sample questions on the book trail

1. Name the country in which Gulliver found himself where the inhabitants were only six inches high.
2. Name three novels about characters called 'Tom'.
3. Which writer was the last winner of the Carnegie Prize?
4. The film *Babe* was based on a book. Name the book and its author.
5. Who created a world carried on the back of four elephants and what is that world called?
6. Who is the woman whose body floats down the river to Camelot?
7. Who wrote the book where time stands still when the clock strikes 13?
8. What are the names of Prospero's servants in Shakespeare's *Tempest*?
9. What is significant about the date that William Shakespeare died?

Local arts organizations may also help with funding of author visits as these are the most costly part. Choosing an author who is only starting to write for young people can be useful as they want to get into schools and fees are not usually as high as for well-established authors.

Timetables

Organizing the timetable is obviously dependent on a number of factors:

- the size of your school;
- the space available;
- the number of authors visiting;
- the number of activities taking place;
- the involvement of other departments.

At a very large comprehensive school it may be difficult to ensure that all students have the opportunity to hear an author speak unless your budget is very large. Then priority needs to be given to students who have studied a book by a particular author or to whose work they have been introduced.

It is important to display the timetable of events prominently so that all staff know what is going on. We have occasionally had staff from other subject areas who have been interested in hearing authors speak.

Staff/student involvement

Planning a whole-school event like this can be very daunting so, if you can, you should co-opt as much help as possible. If other staff and students are involved in the planning, then they feel much more ownership and will throw themselves more wholeheartedly into the Festival. Students can help in the initial stages of trying to decide which authors to invite. You could use a lesson or two for a class to research authors who may be willing to visit. They could:

- find a biography of the author;
- list books written;

- find out something about their genre;
- question students to find any who have read any of these/ find their opinions of them;
- find an extract to read.

They could then present their findings to the rest of the group who then vote on which author to invite. They could then write the invitation. This would ensure an interested audience on the day.

With a large department it is usually easy to co-opt help as no one person then has to be responsible for planning a whole event. A storytelling day was a great example of this. A number of different storytelling groups were invited and the whole Year 8 group was involved. The timetable was collapsed for the day and the students all worked with someone who told them stories, taught them some basic techniques and helped them to develop a story of their own to tell. Classes from the local primary schools were invited for the afternoon and, using the techniques they had learned in the morning, our students told their stories. The planning tasks were split among the department with small groups being responsible for: organizing the primary invitations and arrangements for the visit; the timetable and arranging rooms for these activities; meeting and looking after all our visitors and arranging for their payments. In a smaller English department with fewer staff to help there are other ways you could do this. Liaison with your feeder primary school/s might find you a teacher who would help organize from their end while drama teachers might also want to be involved. You might also want to keep a large event like this separate from a festival week if there are insufficient people to help.

Students usually like to be involved in other ways. Visitors to the school will need looking after during the day and it can be good for this task to be taken on by interested students. It can give them a chance to talk to an author whose work they may have enjoyed on a one to one basis. We had lots of volunteers to take Michelle Magorian round the school and to have lunch with her!

Finally, they can write thank-you letters after the event.

Staff can also be involved with events of their own. An adult book quiz with a book token prize can prove very popular and taxing, yet very entertaining to produce. Book swaps can also get staff talking about their reading preferences too.

Bookfair

Being friends with your local bookshop is useful to you. Hosting a bookshop during the time of the Festival is a good way to encourage readers to become buyers. Most bookshops are keen to make close alliances with schools and will discuss the books that you want them to bring in. They will obviously also know what books sell and can help students to make choices. It may also get you some prizes for competitions. You need to provide somewhere to display the books and a secure place for them. Opening at lunch-times and during breaks allows access to everyone but, if you can staff it, it is also possible to use English lesson time to take classes to visit.

If you don't have a good local bookshop who can come in, Scholastic run book fairs in schools. They bring a wide variety of books. They can be contacted on www.scholastic.co.uk. The website has a link to their book fair service and offers comprehensive help with an organiser's guide which includes advice on what to do:

- before the fair;
- setting up;
- during the fair;
- after the fair.

It also makes clear that up to 60 per cent of the takings can go to the school. Again this can help to fund prizes or visits during the Festival. Although some of the advice is more applicable to primary schools, it can be adapted.

Cross-curricular activities

If you want to take students out of other subjects for events during a Reading Festival it can be good to enlist other curriculum areas into focusing some work during the week for reading-related activities. There are a number of possibilities here.

- Art is an obvious area which easily relates. Fantasy novels can lend themselves to creating unusual characters, settings and creatures. Literary characters have been created by numerous artists and can be used either to study technique or for older students to copy. Poetry is particularly good here and there are a number of books like *Double Vision* by Michael and Peter Benton which links poems and paintings. (I love to combine a reading of U. A. Fanthorpe's 'Not My Best Side' with studying Paolo Uccello's *St George and the Dragon* on National Poetry Day.) Harry Potter would be a rich source of possibilities too.
- Food technology is always inventive. They prepare picnics for Alice and the Famous Five and make biscuits for Winnie the Pooh. I'm sure Jim Crace's *The Devil's Larder* could inspire some interesting work.
- Science/technology could investigate the destruction of cities in *Mortal Engines*. Old science fiction novels would lend themselves to investigation of the accuracy of predictions of the future.
- History uses many of the same books as we do for background reading, so any novel which could link to their current topics could be used. For example:

WWI	Key Stage 3
Remembrance	Theresa Breslin
War Horse	Michael Morpurgo
Private Peaceful	Michael Morpurgo
	Key Stage 4
The Shell House	Linda Newbury
WWII	Key Stage 3
War Boy	Michael Foreman
The Diary of Anne Frank	Anne Frank
Carrie's War	Nina Bawden
Goodnight Mr Tom	Michelle Magorian
The Slave Trade	
Nightjohn	Gary Paulson

American Exploration	Key Stage 3
The Witch of Blackbird Pond	Elizabeth Speare
The Ballad of Lucy Whipple	Karen Cushman
Witch Child	Celia Rees

- Geography could compare settings of novels with their geographical reality. Students can make maps from details given in books or trace routes of journeys. For some writers the sense of place is very strong and recreation in a visual form would be easy. Students could collect their own examples from books they have read. The following lend themselves quite readily to this suggestion.

Little Soldier	Bernard Ashley
Journey to the River Sea	Eva Ibbotson
Trouble Half Way	Jan Mark
The Other Side of Truth	Beverley Naidoo
Witch Child	Celia Rees
Holes	Louis Sachar
The Witch of Blackbird Pond	Elizabeth Speare
The Lord of the Rings	J. R. R. Tolkein

We have also run a very successful evening for staff and parents during the Festival. We invited Wendy Cooling, who has been a teacher, Head of the Children's Book Foundation and is now a freelance book consultant. She came with a huge selection of books which she displayed, described and enthused about. She examined the role of reading and encouraged all those who were there to be adventurous in the texts they offer to students, both those we teach and our own children. Wendy will come into schools for Inset or run evening sessions like the one we had and can be contacted on wendycooling@bookconsult. freeserve.co.uk.

This is not intended to be an exhaustive list of possibilities for a

Reading Festival: I am sure that there are other inventive possibilities for you. Your budget, the number of students and their ages will all put different constraints on you. The most important point is for both you and the students to have fun and to spend some time excitedly talking about books.

6 World Book Day

Another event that can inject fun into the school calendar is World Book Day. This is celebrated each year on the Thursday of the first week in March. This celebration of reading was started in 1998 and is a joint venture between the Publishers' Association and the Booksellers' Association of the UK and Ireland. All school students receive a book voucher for £1 in the week of World Book Day which can be redeemed from participating bookshops. Most large chains and many independent booksellers take part but you should ring your local bookshop to check if they are participating, before recommending them to students.

The tokens can be redeemed towards the cost of any book, usually with a minimum value or can be used to purchase one of the specially written titles. These are often by well-known writers, for example Michael Morpurgo and Eoin Colfer, and the most popular ones can disappear very quickly. On occasions, the six £1 books have topped the *Guardian* bestseller lists. Eoin Colfer's *The Seventh Dwarf* sold 58,000 copies. This demonstrates the large following for junior arch criminal Artemis Fowl. If you use any of the school book clubs, such as Scholastic, students can redeem their tokens as part payment of their order in May which can be useful as it extends the time for students to make decisions.

All schools are sent a Schools Pack which includes a selection of posters advertising the Day, the chosen books and a specific author with recommended reads. Because it is *World* Book Day, Book Aid international is also involved and there are a number of activities and competitions to encourage children to think globally. These are also a rich source of material for assemblies.

I like the comment made by Richard Crabbe, the Chairman of the African Publishers' Network from 1997 to 2002. He says, 'If education is the road out of poverty, books are the wheels needed for the journey'. This was written about the need to support Africa in continuing to develop its educational programmes, but the same message is equally applicable to education everywhere and would provide a useful starting point for the focus of assemblies during the week of World Book Day. The focus on Africa can be accessed through www.bookaid.org. The site introduces some useful ideas which could get students thinking about the wider world and ways in which they can take part. One idea is BookCrossing.

BookCrossing

The website gives more details but essentially this is it:

The 3 Rs of BookCrossing . . .

1. **Read** a good book (you already know how to do that).

2. **Register** it *here* (along with your journal comments), get a unique BCID (**B**ookCrossing **ID** number), and *label the book*.

3. **Release** it for someone else to read (give it to a friend, leave it on a park bench, donate it to charity, 'forget' it in a coffee shop, etc.), and get notified by email each time someone comes here and records journal entries for that book. And if you make *Release Notes* on the book, others can *Go Hunting* for it and try to find it!

The site also has a list of celebrity reading suggestions, many of which could be used to provide readings for assemblies.

Books focused on Africa

The No 1 Ladies' Detective Agency	J. A. McCall Smith
Under My Skin	Doris Lessing
An African Farm	Olive Schreiner
The Poisonwood Bible	Barbara Kingsolver

Don't Let's Go to the Dogs Tonight	Alexandra Fuller
Nervous Conditions	Tsitsi Dangarembga
The Grass is Singing	Doris Lessing
An Ice Cream War	William Boyd
The Famished Road	Ben Okri
The Long Walk to Freedom	Nelson Mandela

Teenage novels

The Garbage King	Elizabeth Laird
Go well, Stay well	Toecky Jones
Skin Deep	Toecky Jones
The Other Side of Truth	Beverly Naidoo

many Nadine Gordimer and Doris Lessing short stories

Also, I like to involve tutors as much as possible. I ask staff either to talk about their current favourite book, the book that has had the greatest impact on them, or their favourite childhood memory of a book, and to read a section to the assembly. Despite some initial resistance, both staff and students enjoy this.

Lessons during the day

The Schools Pack also has a booklet of suggestions for lessons from primary to Key Stage 3. This is a photocopiable resource and is firmly rooted in the Literacy Strategy. Activities range from 'Picture sequencing' through 'Poetry Writing at Key Stage 2' to 'Developing Skills in Reading for KS3 tests', looking at atmosphere and mood in a novel such as *The Ghost Behind the Wall* by Melvin Burgess. These have often proved useful, particularly as a way of introducing tasters of different texts to students.

There is an interesting new activity for 2005. It's called Spread the Word!

'Spread the Word!'

Spread the Word!

I'd like you to read.................because....................

In 2005 World Book Day will be launching an entirely new campaign to encourage people to recommend a good read to friends and family.

Millions of free postcards will be made available throughout the country for you to send with a personal book recommendation – an easy way for everyone to participate in World Book Day.

If you work for an organization that you think might want to get more involved, please contact the *World Book Day Coordinator*.

Many schools use the day itself as a focus for activities centred on reading. Some of the suggestions for events in the Reading Festival section may be appropriate here. Any activity which encourages talk about books is valuable. We usually try to find a method of showing visually the books that students and staff have read. Normally, we start the day with half an hour's private reading, beginning normal lessons at 9.30 am. All staff and students are encouraged to bring in their own reading material for that time and we persuade everyone to take part. Many staff comment on how peaceful a start to the day this makes. Some also take time to discuss their reading habits with students, providing good role models for them. The students do notice which books staff are reading and often take great pleasure in telling me what colleagues are reading.

Each year we create a large display which is in some way related to books. During the day we try to get as many students and staff as possible to add to this with the title and author of the book they have most enjoyed in the previous year. Over the years we have had:

- a large illustration of a bookcase and to this we added small booklike strips with titles;

- a reading tree with leaves in different colours;
- a frog with a heading READ IT (Sorry! The labels with titles were frog-spawn in gaudy colours)
- the year of the dragon was beautiful and we left him up on display for some time – he had scales to show what had been read;
- a bookworm whose head began near the main school entrance and whose segments wound around the whole reception area.

This is the beginning of the day of the dragon. It was painted for us by some Year 12 art students who also happened to be doing A-level English.

The students thoroughly enjoy watching the display fill up and there are always lots of people around it at break and lunch-time discussing what they have put up or filling in their own choices.

Figure 1 Empty dragon

Figure 2 Here's how it looked by the end of the day

I enjoy eavesdropping on this and on the, often heated, discussions in lessons. Staff also join in and their suggestions are often the cause of great interest to students. The discussions often lead to students and staff lending each other favourite books and networks of readers are extended.

When it is all over and we take down the display the titles are checked and counted and the 'Most read book of the year' is displayed in the school resource centre. The top 20 list can also be available to anyone who wants it. This could easily be presented as a bookmark and many students prefer recommendations from other students to the suggestions from teachers. Jacqueline Wilson always comes out top in the list, usually showing nearly ten times more books than any other title. It is also an interesting record of particular enthusiasms. Harry Potter featured heavily three years ago but is dying off now.

It also reflects the way that networking can take place and the results can be a good analysis of the reading taking place in your school. Dave Pelzer's *A Child Called It* has been a popular read among the Years 9 and 10 girls this year, proving to be the most recommended among them while *Artemis Fowl* was very high on the Year 8 boys' list. The suggestion can be useful when deciding what new books to put in book boxes or can reflect, like *Artemis Fowl*, the choices that we have made.

It is also worth tapping into the World Book Day online at www.worldbookdayfestival.com to listen to the writers who are taking part in the Festival. You can access the 2003 and 2004 archives to listen to writers talking about writing and their own reading preferences but on the day itself it is possible to join in with the discussions and to hear the interviews live. The site also provides interesting links to other writing-related activities, for example to the Magic Pencil exhibition which displayed the work of illustrators of children's books. This includes samples of their work and their own comments on their inspiration and methods. Finally there are resources available to download on the authors participating in the online Festival. Some are specific to authors and some are generic activities which could be used as preparation for the interviews on the day itself.

If you organize a whole week of events around World Book Day then many of the suggestions in the Reading Festival chapter may be useful but here are some ideas which might be helpful if you just want to celebrate on that particular day.

- Many schools use this as a good opportunity to invite a writer or a storyteller to the school but you need to organize this at least a year in advance for a popular author.
- Write to parents asking them to contribute to a display of 'The book that hooked me'. These need only be brief but should try to explain why this book had such an effect on them. This could be a homework for students to interview parents and bring in the results, or parents could email them in to school if you have the facility. This could then form part of a permanent display in the reception area as part of creating a reader-friendly school.
- If you are lucky enough to have blocked English lessons you could try swapping classes for each English teacher to present their favourite book or poem to each class. Students could then vote at the end of the lesson for which book/ poem they would choose to read themselves or give to someone as a present.

- Activities in the lunch-time are usually opportunities for fun so this could be an occasion for a book quiz with contestants chosen from each tutor group in a particular year. This would make a good charity event with money given to a local organization.
- The library could have readings from students or staff, or run videos of writers talking. Michael Rosen performing his poetry usually goes down well with Year 7.
- Poetry in performance could also fit in well here. Students could prepare for this in the weeks leading up to World Book Day. If you have a sympathetic headteacher then it could be fun to have a particular year group off timetable for the afternoon to present their performances. This could obviously be developed into something much bigger with other local schools taking part.
- Competitions usually work well too. The art department often helps in judging alternative book covers or bookmarks with winners receiving book tokens.
- Another competition I like the idea of is to match books with members of staff. Interested staff write a brief statement either about their preferred reading or a particular book that they have enjoyed and students have to decide who the books belong to. Again this is an opportunity to involve any staff in the school including those who work in the offices, the canteen or anywhere else on your site. Technologically minded students could take digital photographs for you to display alongside the book descriptions. Again this could be a charitable event with a small sum being charged for entry and book tokens given for the winners.

7 A reading quiz

Many of the issues about reading involve boys. Many of them tend to stop reading, perhaps only for a while though, towards the end of Year 8 if not earlier. Encouraging a strong reading habit which can survive all the other attractions or at least be returned to when a more independent streak takes over from the peer pressure, in later years, is vital. Many of the suggestions for things to do that I have recommended in this book have involved a sense of competitiveness which often appeals to boys. This doesn't, however, put off the girls who cite 'opportunities to read something new and different' as reasons to take part in reading schemes or competitive activities.

This next suggestion has come from Julie Meehan, Expressive Arts Development Officer for Conwy who uses it with primary schools but I can see a wide variety of possible applications for secondary schools. We are a large school with a ten-group intake that is taught as mixed-ability tutor groups for English in Year 7 which is where, I think, I would initially aim this.

The idea is to have a reading quiz and performance day. So, here is my suggestion for its use.

Step 1
You need an enthusiastic group of interested staff to set up and run this. Their first task would be to choose a number of novels which are to be used as the basis of the quiz:

- these could be new novels that have recently come out;
- a selection of stock that the department already has available;
- prize winners; or
- any theme that you might be using as a departmental scheme of work.

Ideally they should cover a range of ability so that all students can participate.

Step 2

The staff need to read all of these books between them and should undertake to write a series of quiz questions on them which should be sufficiently testing to need quite a detailed knowledge of the text. This could, incidentally, make a good activity for World Book Day which is usually about the middle of March, so I would begin with the staff reading the books over the Christmas holidays.

Step 3

Each group would then be given a set of the books and the date of the quiz so that they know how long they have to read them:

- this could involve interested volunteers who make up a small team;
- or if you are using texts of which you already have copies, all students could choose one of the books to read;
- if as many students as possible read the texts, then they can choose their own team.

Step 4

The next part of the exercise is to provide a dramatized performance of the text or some section of it. This should last no longer than five minutes, and is a good way of involving students who would not necessarily choose to read for a quiz:

- a team of perhaps six or eight readers will each read at least two of the chosen books;
- two students who have read the same text will then work with a group to prepare this performance;
- they can choose some sections to read to their group and the group then prepare their drama.

This encourages closer readings of texts and, as it is students who explain the details, these act as good role models for others in the class. It is particularly good for boys who are readers to gain status for it and to help others to take a more active interest.

Here you could enlist the support of any drama teachers. Your staff group could suggest passages of the text which might dramatize well or give ideas to dramatize the whole texts. In many schools this is often a term when there are ITE students in school and this can often mean the opportunity to team teach classes or allow staff on the teacher group to visit and support teachers who are less familiar with the texts.

Dramatizing suggestions

- Imagine a television or film version of the book has just been released and create the trailer for it.
- Act out a particularly interesting or exciting section ending with a cliffhanger so that the audience needs to read the book to find out what happens.
- Produce a dramatized reading using freeze-frames or tableaux.
- Prepare an interview with characters from the book and/ or the author.

Students need time to work on their presentations and can be encouraged to find music and costumes to support them. With a large year group it would be necessary for each tutor group to decide which performance would go through to the final that will be adjudicated on the day.

Step 5

You now need a sympathetic headteacher who will let you collapse the timetable for Year 7 for a day, that's why World Book Day seems such a good idea.

- The quiz takes place during the first part of the morning, either as a pub quiz with all the questions on paper for the teams to answer while the other students put the finishing touches to their performances.
- Or with the whole year group watching and encouraging their team.

Again this would work better if a large number of students have
read the books.

- After the quiz is finished the performances can begin and,
  even at five minutes per piece, this will take a couple of
  hours with a large year group.
- You could devise a points system with each tutor group
  voting.
- Or you could give the proceedings added weight by having a
  panel of judges.

If you have been lucky enough to involve other staff, i.e. dance,
music or drama departments, you could invite them to do the
adjudication. The points from the quiz and the performance are
then added and prizes are given, perhaps a book token to be spent
on books of their choice by the tutor group.

Another way of using the same idea would be to adapt it to use
as a primary liaison activity. Year 6 in your feeder schools could be
invited to take part using a similar procedure, along with students
in Year 7. In a small school all Year 7 classes could be involved
and this would make a good activity towards the end of the
summer term after Key Stage 2 SATs have been completed.

8 Books over Breakfast

Reluctant readers

Students arriving at secondary school after a six-week summer break often go backwards in their reading ability. The more reluctant readers may not have picked up a book in that time and are past the age when parents still read to them, so stories on paper may have lost their ability to engage them. Their confidence may have dwindled too so that the demands of the average secondary-school curriculum may become a great challenge. Differentiated work can help this but ideally students should be given strategies and the confidence to help them to tackle challenging texts both in academic areas and in their own reading choices.

Reluctant readers come in many forms. Some don't have the facility to decode text and are reluctant because the act of trying to decode is very difficult for them. The scope of this book does not include the excellent work carried out in special needs departments to improve the reading scores of the weakest students but there are reluctant readers of a different sort whom we can address. Reading for pleasure and reading for learning should not be completely separate skills, yet many students that you teach do make this distinction. They will say that they 'don't like reading' or 'they never read'. What they mean is that they never choose a book as a form of entertainment. For some it is because of their lack of facility in reading, but for others it is more a lack of investment in the necessary practice to make a real difference to their facility. For these sort of students there are any number of cross-over schemes such as Books over Breakfast and Paired Reading Schemes which aim to:

- improve reading skills;
- encourage pleasure in reading texts.

As we are a community school, the funding for our Books over Breakfast scheme has been from community education. Many schools use such schemes where students come in to have breakfast and to enhance their learning. The one I want to describe is not the only way, but it does work, and can be adapted to suit the circumstances of your own school. Its aim is to boost confidence for all readers and to provide one-to-one attention for readers to help them to improve.

Letters are sent at the beginning of the autumn term to the parents of Year 7 students telling them all about the scheme and inviting them to encourage their children to take part. The member of staff in charge then visits a Year 7 assembly to advertise the programme. Finally, Year 7 students all take a London reading test in the first week in our school and all those students with a reading score of below 90 are invited individually to attend. However, pressure is not put on them to attend; all those who attend are volunteers and self-selected by attendance. Most are students who need to improve their reading levels but some continue to come because they enjoy the opportunity.

Training helpers

Another appeal of a scheme such as this is the sixth-form helpers who work with individual students on a regular basis. The helpers attend regularly and are there for a variety of reasons. Some want to work with children or be teachers themselves; one of our students came because his little brother came and he liked the idea of helping others, as his brother was being helped. Many attend a course on learning to support readers. They role-play situations to learn techniques to support readers with encouragement and challenge. The emphasis is on praise to help to boost confidence and to increase the willingness to attempt more challenging texts. This demonstrates real commitment from the sixth form, many of whom attend for the whole of their two-year course. The younger students like the regular contact and do form a strong bond with the older ones. The youngsters feel very safe with them and say that 'he makes me feel more confident about my reading' and 'I don't mind making mistakes because she always helps me and I don't feel stupid'. They like the technique of someone reading along with them, then gradually stopping as they develop confidence. This one-to-one support scaffolds their own skill and provides a safety net for problem words.

Meetings

The meetings are held twice a week starting at 8 am, and we are lucky enough to have a community lounge with kitchen facilities which is where the students meet. Breakfast is cereal, toast with chocolate spread and hot drinks, usually hot chocolate. One student says he only came in the beginning 'for the Coco Pops'. It doesn't matter if this is the case because the reading still gets done and the improvements are made, although incidentally rather than purposely.

There is a selection of comics and magazines for them to read while eating their breakfast and this is also a chat time to catch up on the news with their partners. The social aspects of a group like this are obviously important too. 'I like to come and meet my friends' and 'we have a good laugh'. Many of these students would not have breakfast if it is not provided and a friendly face in the upper years of the school is often very important to them. Most of the sixth formers are girls, but there are boys too and these are tremendously good role models for some of the younger ones, particularly as many of those who attend are boys. Recent research demonstrates that boys do lag behind in their reading and the title of this book implies that 'the buggers' don't want to read, but this scheme shows that a number of students are aware of their limitations and are prepared to take steps to improve. It is interesting that it is mostly boys who recognize this and are actively doing something about it. The take-up of the Books over Breakfast scheme demonstrates this. Some of the students are there because their parents encourage them: 'When the letter came from school saying that there were two ways I could work on my reading, miss some lessons for extra help, or go to Books over Breakfast my Mum didn't want me to miss lessons'. You could argue that their parents have put pressure on them to attend but this would not account for their continued attendance. Although numbers do dwindle towards the end of the year some students continue into Year 8.

At 8.30 am the group move to the resource centre for the more formal part of the meeting. Here the students choose the books they want to read from a wide selection of fiction and non-fiction and settle down with their partners. They read for 20 minutes or so and are encouraged by their partners. Their progress is charted quite informally with a card and sticker system which keeps a record of the number of books read and the type. The stickers can be exchanged for vouchers when a personal target of stickers is reached.

Most of those who attend can see the difference it has made to their reading. They are aware that they are more confident both in reading alone and, more importantly for them, in reading aloud in class. A number report that now they will volunteer to read sometimes whereas they used to hate it, particularly when 'other kids used to laugh because I stumbled over words'. One boy was proud that he now only makes mistakes over names that he hasn't heard before. Another was able to tell a story about his own miscue where he read 'prostitute' instead of Protestant. He said that everyone laughed but it was all right 'because it was a mistake that anyone could make'.

Some report that now they will choose a book to read in private reading lessons and feel happy to concentrate on that. For many it is non-fiction that appeals and they are pleased when their choice of books can also help in other subjects – often history because of the appeal of the Horrible History series.

Paired reading

The process used by the sixth-form students includes paired reading, but I want to look more closely at the method and suggest ways of using it to make real improvements in students' reading abilities. Like any reading improvement scheme, paired reading targets specific students. Most secondary schools carry out some standardized test of reading ability when students arrive. This is then used, in conjunction with primary school records, to determine which students are in need of some form of intervention. In general a notional reading age of 9.5 years is necessary to ensure that students can access the curriculum. Obviously this is only a guideline and many of the materials you use will expect a higher reading ability than this, particularly if you use newspaper articles from broadsheet newspapers. For this reason a reading age of 9.5 or below is the level at which most schools will try to intervene.

The process of paired reading was initially developed as a method for parents to use at home with their children. Its main purpose is to improve the competence and confidence of readers and can be used at any level of reading and with any age reader. It specifically allows readers to tackle texts which are beyond their level of independent reading and gives them support in doing so. Children who have taken part in the process like it as it makes them feel in control and all the studies which have been done show an increase in the children's reading fluency and accuracy. Our own experience with the Books over Breakfast group bears this out.

First of all let me describe the process. When the students and their partners meet for the first time they agree on a signal to start reading. This can be anything; the student may initiate it orally, 'Shall we start now?' or a signal like a tap on the arm can be given but both student and partner need to be clear as to what it is. They also need to agree a signal for the student to begin reading solo. On this first meeting the partner needs to explain carefully how the technique works. The reading material is chosen by the student and can be changed at any time. The choices have to be carefully worked out to be within their reading abilities. There are now many more reading books designed for lower reading ages which are closely related to interest levels of older students which make it easier to select appropriate material.

Choosing texts

Some publishers like Barrington Stoke use young people to try out their books before publication. It is possible through their website to enrol students to become consultants for them. They are sent books to read and asked to comment when they have finished. The students' comments are taken into consideration before the final version of the book is agreed and all student consultants are given a free copy of the published book with their names inscribed in the front.

They have also engaged popular and favourite writers like Michael Morpurgo and Malorie Blackman to contribute to their catalogues. The book lists specify age level for interest and reading ages to help choices. For example:

Ghost for Sale	Terry Deary
Bungee Hero	Julie Bertagna
Starship Rescue	Theresa Breslin
Hostage	Malorie Blackman
Tod in Biker City	Antony Masters
Wartman	Michael Morpurgo

Other publishers like Franklin Watts concentrate on non-fiction texts, often popular with reluctant readers, again with specified age-range interest levels:

Extreme sports
In-line skating   Mountain biking   Skateboarding

Get real
Daring escapes   Football heroes   Mountain horror

When the students have chosen their books you need to supply a quiet place without distractions and sufficient time to allow them both to relax and enjoy the experience. It doesn't need long time stretches: ten to 15 minutes is usually enough to maintain the attention span. Some schools build a programme into PSHE time, while others use lunch-times or before-school slots.

The reading begins in duet. The student may set the pace or the partner can be very slightly ahead to support the more hesitant reader. If an error is made it is important that the correction is non-critical; the partner says the word and the student repeats it. When the signal is given to go solo the partner should praise the student who can continue for as long as he/she wants. Support and praise should continue to be given when they read alone. When a mistake is made the partner corrects it and the reading continues in duet until the student gives the signal again.

This may sound very prescriptive, but the format provides real comfort and support for struggling readers and has a highly beneficial effect on their reading scores.

I have described this as an initiative which a whole school might take to improve the reading of their students but there are other ways of using it. If you are working on a book and you want the students to read, you could choose sympathetic pairings and encourage students to read together. They could determine the criteria for support as a group before you begin so that sympathetic reading is carried out. You might need to streamline the system a little, removing the going solo signals and continuing duet reading for your specified period of time.

If you use any of the reading challenges or private reading sessions this could again be adapted for use in encouraging the more reluctant readers to engage with the tasks.

Part Two

In the Classroom

9 The reader-friendly classroom

If you are as curious as most English teachers are you will know that moment when you first visit a new friend's house and you surreptitiously look around to see where the books are and occasionally gravitate towards them. This invariably starts conversations about recently enjoyed books and can often help to cement friendships.

Display

Students need to feel that same sense that books are valued when they enter a classroom for their first English lesson of a new school year. If they have not been in your room before, their first impression is doubly important because it says a good deal about you and your values. The displays on your walls are the first things that they notice so they should reflect and stimulate both your and your students' interests. Students work is the best way to let students see what is expected of them. What you choose to put on the wall shows them the quality and type of work that they are going to be asked to do. If the quality is good, with care being taken over presentation, then they realize that these are your expectations of them.

Work done by other students is an important source of reading material in a classroom, particularly for more reluctant readers. You will have found this whenever you change a display; students are always drawn to it and read what is there, particularly if it is the same work that they themselves have done when they were younger or that they might do later. This stimulates discussion and reminiscence involving most of the class and provides opportunities to reflect on the ways in which they have changed and the differences in the quality of their writing now. Seeing how far they have come helps to consolidate their gains, making them conscious and explicit. It also works in the opposite direction, creating aspirations. For example, one Year 11 student said 'Does everyone in the sixth form do that?' on a display about Gothic literature which opened a discussion on possible A-level texts, always useful when Year 11 are beginning to think about making choices.

Other display material can be anything colourful which might stimulate discussion.

- Postcards which you add to and change regularly are a rich source of discussion and writing focus.
- Posters advertising films, plays, books and authors all encourage talk, often critical, of current enthusiasms.
- Book posters do need to be changed regularly. If you use Scholastic, then you may receive posters with your orders. Sometimes there are poetry posters for sale in their teachers' resource leaflets. Making friends with your local bookshop can help too. I had a cardboard cut-out of the car from Harry Potter's *Chamber of Secrets* hanging from my ceiling for a while when the book first came out.
- Film posters promote discussion of favourite characters and debates on which they prefer, the book or the film. They are also models for creating their own film posters for books studied in class and for media study at Key Stage 3 and GCSE.
- Important reference material displayed in an accessible and eye-catching way.

The next most important area is the supply of books around the room. All English classrooms need a supply of good teenage and young adult fiction and some time should be given over to introducing new classes to this supply. There are myriad ways that you can do this and here are some that have worked for me.

Put out on the desks all the reading books in the room. They should not be grouped in any way. Put students into twos or threes and ask them to do one of the following activities:

- Give each pair a different genre: horror, fantasy, animal stories, family stories, school stories, science fiction, romance, historical and ask them to collect as many books as they can which fit that genre using only the title and the front cover. They then present their criteria for judgement to the rest of the class. They can then read the blurbs to see if these bear out their initial judgements.
- Ask the students to circulate and to pick out any books that they have read. Depending on the number of books you have, you can give them a number to select. They should then put these in the order of the ones liked most to least and explain their reasons to the rest of the class. (For those students who are not great readers it is important to have some film tie-ins, some graphic novels and series like the Horrible Histories which they may have dipped into.)
- Ask the students to choose a book that they would like to read based only on the cover and to justify their choice.
- Ask the students to choose a book that they think another student in the class would like to read and explain why.

This can also be a way of weeding out books at the end of a year. Keen readers in the classroom can help decide which books they have not enjoyed or would never choose to read. If you have students with wide enough genre tastes this can be a very revealing exercise.

Reading influences

Once you have introduced new students to what is available in your room, you need to help them broaden their means of making choices. As adults, we choose what we are going to read in numerous ways:

- recommended by friends and family/borrowed from them;
- reviews in the press, radio and TV;
- dramatizations on TV or the radio;

- reading groups;
- knowledge of the author's previous works;
- browsing in a bookshop;
- given as presents;
- from the library;
- advertisements in shops/magazines/newspapers.

Our students need to be confident in using these same systems to enable them to make wide choices with a good hope of success. Many young people do turn to some of these naturally and our job is to try to encourage them to take advantage of the other methods to help them to try a wider range of styles and a cross-section of different genres. Although reading one genre is common to many readers, both adults and students alike, it is better to arrive there as a result of discrimination rather than by default and being open to the suggestions around them may help to find that position.

When you talk to your students about making choices about what to read you will find many of them are quite conservative. Their parents figure strongly, mainly because these are the people who buy books for them or take them to the library. This can be quite passive: books 'are bought for me so I don't have to spend any money that way'. Or 'my Mum's good at choosing for me and it is hassle-free.' Other parents do challenge their children's expectations: 'My Mum usually buys for me and she chooses ones I wouldn't but I always enjoy them'. Unfortunately they don't always get it right, sometimes having higher aspirations than the students can cope with. 'I prefer to buy them myself as sometimes they are bought for me and they are a bit too old.' Notice all these comments are about buying or having books bought for them. Many students say that their parents will willingly buy them books, although other requests aren't as readily fulfilled.

Most students seem to prefer to own books, no surprise there, I do too. Some like the ability to choose 'the genre I like', some want to 'read them again', while others like the feel and look of new books 'as the pages feel less dry' and 'the covers are shiny and it's better to have really nice-looking book on your shelf than an old one'. For many too, the time element is important. 'I can take as long as I like.' With some saying that they don't like having to give back a book that they have really enjoyed.

For some however, the library is a godsend as 'there is a lot of choice' and 'I don't have to pay anything'. For readers whose parents don't have the necessary disposable income or for whom reading is not a habit, access to a library whether it is in the English classroom or elsewhere in the school, is essential. This is where school reading schemes are useful but I will deal with this elsewhere.

Friends are also a useful influence. 'I prefer to borrow from friends because they know it's good.' 'Recommendations from friends make me confident in what I buy.' Some students trust their friends' judgement and like to try out books or writers 'to see if I like it', knowing too that 'most of my friends and me have lots in common and like the same stuff'.

My friends and I have a very strong networking system with books. I know whose judgement I can rely on and who will introduce me to something new that I might not otherwise have tried. The biggest single factor in making this work is opportunity to chat. I have colleagues who I always chat to in passing to see what they have read over the holidays and friends who I know will always have enjoyed the same books as me and like to discuss them. In class we need to introduce students to ways of finding networks of their own to encourage them to try a greater variety of texts. If you have a lesson, or at least some time set aside for silent reading, it is worth using this occasionally to showcase what students are reading. Sometimes I use this with a class at the beginning of the year to help me to learn a little about the students and to help to remember their names, a vital thing to do quickly to help classroom management. I give the students a few minutes to think about the book or film that they have enjoyed most over the summer holidays. It is important to include films for those who won't have read a book. I then model for them by talking about something I have enjoyed, explaining where I was when I read it and why it has made an impact on me. I try to choose something that I know some of them may have read, a new book in a series or by a popular author or a film tie-in. I then invite them to introduce themselves and their subject. I try to note what they tell me as it is a useful indicator of their reading interests and levels. Many students then join in the discussion if it is something that they too have seen or read. This is also a good opportunity for them to suggest titles for me. In the same way that when they enjoy something that you have recommended it creates trust, they gain confidence from suggesting titles to you and discussing them with you afterwards. It is a useful way to tap in to what is currently popular. I found Garth Nix's *Sabriel* through a student recommendation this way.

Using a book club like Scholastic, who send out leaflets, is also a way of allowing students the opportunity to discuss their reading. (I will deal more fully with the use of book clubs elsewhere.) When the leaflets arrive we spend some time looking through them to see if there if anything that anyone has read and could recommend. This usually brings up other books by the same author which have been enjoyed and gives me suggestions for titles to add to the classroom library. Incidentally, it also gives some money to spend there too.

I allow books to be borrowed from my library too, and keep a notebook to monitor who has borrowed something. A few minutes spent at the beginning or end of the lesson to take out and return books invariably involves the students and me in a discussion of what they have just read. This ensures that certain books are spread more widely. *The Thief Lord* by Cornelia Funke has been taken out by nearly one third of one class purely by this word of mouth recommendation, as has Malorie Blackman's *Noughts and Crosses*.

Television or film tie-ins are also useful talking points. Inevitably *The Lord of the Rings* and Harry Potter have made the biggest impact in recent years with many students attempting to read Tolkien who would not have otherwise have done so, often encouraged by others who have finished the trilogy talking about the books. Anne Fine is another useful example of this as a number of her books have been made into TV series or films. A discussion of why the title of *Madame Doubtfire* was changed to *Mrs Doubtfire* introduced a number of students to the book while the recent series of *Feather Boy* on TV encouraged a number of students to read it.

Choosing books

All those who are let loose in a bookshop with a generous adult, with pocket money, with birthday gift tokens or those who spend time in the library (class, school or public) have the same decisions to make about how to decide whether the book they take from the shelf will appeal to them or not so we need to help to equip them with some ways of making judgements which will stand them in good stead.

Looking carefully at book covers is a useful exercise for students. Many are very influenced by them, particularly when they are strongly involved with a particular genre. They say that the cover has a powerful influence on them 'because it explains the book and lets me know what sort of story it is going to be', or that the cover shows them 'what characters are in it'. Colourful covers which 'are bright and interesting' and which immediately attract attention are important. Boring covers suggest that 'the book won't be very good either'. Some, however, do realize that they are not necessarily a reflection of what is inside and use other techniques to decide on what to read.

Other books by the same author are an important influence too. Readers like to feel safe and know that they will enjoy the book before they start; tried and tested authors ensure that this will happen. Reading books by the same author can be satisfying for a number of reasons: 'The author can also indicate the genre of a certain book, enabling you to read similar books of the same subject'; 'The author influences me as if I like an author's style of writing I usually like the rest of his/her work'. And 'I usually like the same thing the author writes.' Sometimes it is because of continuations. Students who wait avidly for the next Harry Potter want to know what will happen to him and his friends. They empathize with the characters and see them as 'friends' whose well-being is important. Often what happens in the story is less relevant than 'who dies' and who the love interest is. It is an interesting reflection on the perceived reading habits of young people that in the past parents were sometimes concerned that their children seem to get stuck in a particular series and only read within it. Enid Blyton's *Famous Five*, *Sweet Valley High* or *Point Horror* came in for a great deal of criticism at various points in the past. Now society seems very grateful to J. K. Rowling for 'hooking' young readers into a series which will keep them reading.

Of course your own recommendations are very important to

many students. Many of them want to widen the scope of their reading, but don't know where to go next. Once you find something that you have enjoyed which they read and like, you are in and they will listen to you and try books and writers that you recommend. *Coram Boy* went down well with a small group of Year 9 students last year in just this way. Some went on to read *The True Confession of Charlotte Doyle*, *Witch Child* and *Chinese Cinderella* as a consequence of liking my initial suggestions. It does mean that a large part of your own reading needs to keep up with new books that come out, but in term-time that's sometimes no bad thing as they're quick and usually a relatively easy read.

More reluctant readers

All of this works well with students who are already readers, but as we all know a number of students will not pick up a book by choice. We need to encourage students to bring in their own books not only for private reading sessions but for odd moments spare at the ends of lessons or when tasks are completed. However, there are students who not only are not reading anything at home but who cannot really conceive why they should want to. There are countless reasons why this might be so:

- there may be no reading culture in their home, perhaps a few magazines and the sports pages of newspapers only;
- learning to read may have been difficult, so books are not associated with pleasure or entertainment;
- they may find it difficult to make pictures in their heads from the words that they read;
- pleasure in stories is only associated with visual representations;
- fiction has little appeal; only non-fiction on subjects which don't always receive adult approval appeals.

It is all very well for us as English teachers to provide the books that we, and sometimes the government, approve of but, if we are to encourage all students to read, then our classrooms need to include material that they will read. The most obvious way to do this is to talk to your students, not only about the books that you want to buy for your room, but also about what else they would like to see there. The first starting point is graphic novels and comics. *The Simpsons* comic books are always sought out in my room and knowledgeable discussions take place in comparing these with the television series.

The issue of magazines can be a little more of a problem, particularly with the explicit sexual nature of many of the magazines read by young teenage girls. You can get round it by supplying magazines on requested subjects yourself. Many students have very specific interests, particularly in what some would call the more borderline sports and these can be a good source of reading material for students who don't normally read books. A well-resourced library can be very helpful here and these will often be able to keep more up to date than you. It can also provide daily and local newspapers which can stimulate the interests of reluctant fiction readers. A colleague in the science department has recently supplied a pile of fishing magazines which are read avidly by some boys who otherwise find it difficult to settle.

A wide selection of non-fiction is also important. Interests go in phases; currently my students are hooked on *The Guinness Book of World Records*. The extremes of the physical condition shown always fascinate them. This is echoed by the interest shown in any true-life stories, mysteries, crimes or supernatural experiences, so a selection of these, preferably illustrated, is always useful.

Another popular addition to the reading shelf is that of the 'Choose your own adventure' series. These have become much more widely enjoyed again, so it is important to keep dice in your room so that choices can be made. Some boys like the fact that the story is never the same for two people, while others see the small quantity of text as not as daunting as a 'whole book to be got through'. It also has strong links with the computer games that they play but more of that in Chapter 13, Computers and reading.

The area that I have not yet talked about is poetry. Having a selection of poetry books in your room is essential. Some students will claim to dislike it, particularly if they feel that they are going to have to study it. Many know that they won't 'get what it's all about', suggesting that poets make things difficult deliberately to confuse them, but a brightly coloured anthology with a user-friendly title – *My Grannie is a Sumo Wrestler*, *The Spot on my Bum*, or *Poems with Attitude* – have more appeal. Often when students are struggling to find something to read in the classroom, I read them Andrew Fusek Peter's poems, 'Sugar and Spice' and 'Slugs and Snails'. They like the subversion and the 'rudeness' of a poem that mentions farts and the book quickly disappears. Some students read the whole collection over a couple of weeks or take it home to finish.

The most important point in all of this is that we need to ask our students, listen to their responses and act on them. If they are to become critical readers in their own right then they must be aware that their choices are valid and can be used to inform what happens in the classroom. If we can do this then they become partners in the reading process and advances are made in their skills.

10 Class libraries/book boxes

We should remember why we, as adults, read: for pleasure, entertainment, knowledge and information, to make sense of the world around us, to help us go to sleep, to keep us awake, to relieve boring train journeys, to allow us to experience fear and excitement in a controlled environment; the list is endless. We need to encourage our students too to see reading as an experience to accompany them throughout their lives, playing diverse roles, as well as providing textual extracts to analyse. To do this they need to be supported in choosing books which will develop their reading skills and which will help to widen their range of choices.

There are plenty of ways that you can do this:

- have a well-chosen class library;
- visit the school library purposefully;
- run reading schemes;
- use book clubs and/or book fairs.

Choosing books for a class library

Classroom book boxes complement libraries and help to encourage students to make discriminating choices in their own purchases by introducing them to new authors or genres. If your school does not have classroom libraries and you are starting from scratch you should have fun. Use the students first to say what they would like to see there. If it is a mixed-ability group, then you will get a good cross-section of ideas which is useful to ensure that there is something for everyone. This will probably include some graphic novels as well as non-fiction reflecting current enthusiasms. Then you can get help in making choices from a selection of publications.

- *NATE News* is always a source of reviews of teenage literature. You can access their website even if you aren't a member. New fiction is regularly reviewed at www.nate.org.uk.
- Many newspapers review selections on a weekly basis, e.g. the *Guardian* at www.books.guardian.co.uk/reviews/ or the *Independent* at www.enjoyment.independent.co.uk then Enjoyment→Books→Reviews→Teenage Fiction. Teenage Fiction reviewed is currently found on page 10.
- Booklists for Young Adults on the Web is a useful website which helps you or your students to find other books which might reflect their interests. It has an 'If you liked this, try this section'. It is at www.seemore.mi.org/booklists/.
- The Federation of Children's Book Groups also produces a series of booklists for students at different ages, e.g. Picture books, Books to Share, Confident Readers, Teenage Novels, Non-Fiction and Poetry books. Their website is at www.fcbg.org.uk.

Needless to say this is not a definitive list. Any trawl through websites with children and reading in the title will probably throw up some suggestions. Also your local bookshop will usually be helpful both in making suggestions based on their knowledge of the books and of what is popular among the different age groups. Of course budgets will affect your decision of what to buy, and here running a school book club like Scholastic can be very helpful as the books are discounted to the students and you are given free book vouchers dependent on the number of books you buy.

When choosing books for your classroom you do face some dilemmas. In our resource centre books are categorized according to their genre, but also according to age group. Teenage novels aimed at the 14-plus group are categorized as 'young adult' and these may have a more explicit content either in dealing with relationships, in the language that they use or in the level of violence. For example, *Junk* and *Lady* by Melvyn Burgess, *Across the Nightingale Floor* by Lian Hearn, *Troy* by Adele Geras and *Postcards from No-Man's Land* by Aidan Chambers all fall into the young adult category. These are all books which have been recommended in various publications and which are enjoyed by many young people. Because the libraries designate them for older readers, parents can tell immediately that their content may be unsuitable for 11- or 12-year-old students. You then have to decide how to manage this in a classroom. Do you choose only to have non-controversial books, do you refuse to lend them to younger ones, or do you separate them from the rest of the books in your room? This is an issue you need to resolve at departmental level, if you choose to have some of the more controversial books like *Junk*. It may be enough for you to gently steer younger readers away from them or, more explicitly, steer them to books which are more appropriate for their age group. If this sounds suspiciously like censorship I suppose it is. I do think that there is a difference in students choosing from a library books which are clearly designated as being for an older audience and my allowing them to take books to which I know that some parents could have legitimate objections. Of course, the knowledge that some people would not like them to read a certain book makes it even more attractive. I always tell my students that if *Romeo and Juliet* were a modern play with the equivalent in rude jokes and concentration on passion and violence, we would not be encouraged to study it at Years 9 or 10. Looking for the rude jokes concentrates their minds when we read it.

I often get round the issue of censorship by discussing it with students. I always ask what their parents feel about their reading material. Many say that their parents don't mind what they read and, judging by some of the texts that young people have borrowed from Mum or Dad, this is obviously true. For those who say that their parents exercise some form of discrimination for them, I suggest that they talk about the book with their parents, reporting my concerns, showing them the blurb and enlisting their involvement.

With that problem out of the way you can go on your spending spree. The English teacher in me knows the books which we should have on our shelves, the books which win the awards, the classics that the National Curriculum says that they should read and the ones which the Library Association recommend, and there are many readers who will lap these up, returning for more every private reading session. For these readers, the latest Garth Nix, Tim Bowler or Philip Pullman will always be a draw.

However, we always have a number of students for whom these are too challenging and with Paul Jennings's comment on how we have just not found the right book for reluctant readers, we need to reflect the tastes and abilities of these students too. Girls are easier: Jacqueline Wilson rarely fails to please and a wide selection of her books is always useful, as are the 'Ally's World' series. Chick lit has found its way in here too and Books like *Angus, Thongs and Full Frontal Snogging* by Louise Rennison are readily snapped up by Year 8. The most difficult group to satisfy are those who never read anything. For some, reading holds no pleasure, often because it is too difficult. While this can be addressed in other ways, for example paired reading sessions (described elsewhere in this book), I think it is still important to have material in a class library which they can read and find satisfying. This group has perhaps the most specific taste: it must be exciting, easy to read, have pictures too, and be up-to-date and attractive-looking. A good reader will accept that a dull outdated cover can still contain a good story, but the weaker ones need bright, colourful, sparky covers to make them even take the book from the shelf. My students' current favourites are *The Simpsons* comic books and *The Guinness Book of World Records*.

One final point to be aware of is bilingual readers. These can range from Gujerati to Finnish in any large comprehensive school. If you know that you have a student in your class who is bilingual it is interesting to see the response if you offer them some material in their own language. Sometimes they will help by bringing in their own texts once they realize that they are encouraged to do so. This always stimulates discussion among other students, particularly if the text is one that they have read themselves. We had fun with a *Point Horror* in French!

Comics

The issue of reading comics is also one which we could address here. It is easy to dismiss comics as having little or no value to a developing reader and as things which have no real place in school. Many teachers are uncomfortable with them, citing the high levels of violence and lack of continuous text as reasons not to allow them as reading material in classrooms. The images of some, such as *Wonder Woman*, are seen as sensational and explicitly sexual while in others, such as *The Simpsons*, the language is often crude and challenging towards authority.

If we find space in class for encouraging private reading it is important not to exclude some readers. Reading comics also fulfils a very specific function for some students. It may be a link to a more grown-up world and is often a source of discussion in families. Some students like the fact that their 'Dad always reads my *Beano*. He laughs at the same things I do'. In a discussion about comics a mixed group of Year 8 students talked about their reading of them.

Student One: I always used to borrow my brother's.

Student Two: Yes, so did I and we used to talk about them and laugh at what they did.

Student Three: When I went to school they had them there and we used to sit and read together in a group. They had old ones from about 1987 and stuff like that. The older ones were different but I preferred the newer ones because they had colour.

Having reading models is very important, particularly for teenage boys. For many of them, stories are associated with the females in the house. Many more mothers then fathers traditionally read to their children and, as children grow older, they see mothers reading novels while many fathers have little time for books. They may read newspapers regularly and perhaps novels only on holiday. For some teenage boys, reading can seem a female activity and, as they want to define their association with the masculine role, even good readers reject stories. Comics can be a way into a shared world with brothers and fathers which maintains their reading practice.

As student three says above, reading comics can also be a group activity. They sometimes took roles and read them like a play script. Shared enjoyment of a text is an important factor in continuing to read and in creating a willingness to attempt more unknown material. This is also seen where the students had comics in their language classes. Knowing the stories and the characters developed their understanding in the foreign language and made them more confident.

Student Two: We had them in German too. I learned to say 'Eat my shorts' in German.

Two more students were interested in the change of comics over generations.

Student Four: My Granddad was sorting out the attic and he found all my Dad's old *Beano* comics.

Student Three: They've changed since then but not much. They've introduced newer characters and they're more colourful, but Dennis the Menace is still there.

He was interested in the fact that his Dad had kept his comics and that his Grandad had stored them in the attic rather than throwing them away. This gave the comics reading status in their eyes and they enjoyed comparing the old ones with the more modern editions. They made judgements about the style and types of stories, aware of the effect of colour in making stories 'seem more real' and of the way in which, in stories with lots of colour, 'your eyes are drawn to them and you want to read what's there'.

Much of the recent research reported by the Literacy Trust suggests that 'enthusiasm about reading a range of diverse material is a more important factor in success in literacy at age 15 than having well-educated parents in good jobs'. Another study confirms that the interest in reading in free time and the breadth of materials, newspapers, books, magazines and comics read is closely linked to the performance of 16 year olds in areas of reading literacy. This enthusiasm can be developed with students reading to others as well as themselves:

Student Five: I read them to my little brother 'cos he always wanted my Mum to read them and she got fed up with them but I didn't mind 'cos they're easy to read. There's no complicated language in them and they're funny.

This attitude keeps this particular student reading and maintains a strong relationship with a smaller brother. It also sends an important message about reading to the younger child and reinforces the model of reading enjoyment that we want to encourage. When we choose to run reading schemes or challenges we often set homework of reading aloud and the listener has to mark the reading record as in primary school. Many students then read to younger siblings and the comments show how enjoyable both children find that.

Another criticism of comics is the fact that the stories are often anarchic; the challenge to authority worries parents and teachers who think that children will copy the activities they see in the comics, but the students are well aware of the fantasy element of the characters' 'naughty' actions. They know that the stories represent patterns of behaviour that don't usually happen. 'You don't see little boys in the street throwing stones at Grandma.' And they know that this is unacceptable but there is humour in the knowledge that it is 'someone else doing it and it's not you getting into trouble and that makes you laugh'.

There are two distinct strands here: naughty things that you wouldn't do but deep down you might quite like to try, and the element of enjoying watching other people get into trouble for some reason. When the students identify with the latter situation they are recognizing the age-old enjoyment in the pleasure to be gained from other people's misfortunes as most of us do when we watch slapstick comedy routines. These elements of vicarious pleasure are also useful yardsticks when we are choosing texts for private reading shelves and account for a great deal of the popularity of writers of comedy such as Paul Jennings and, to a certain extent, seeing the tribulations of the Baudelaires in Lemony Snicket's books.

Another counter-argument used by students to respond to the suggestion that comics are a bad influence is that so many of the stories have a strong moral message. The students interviewed cited particular instances where 'bad baby people who had done something wrong' are punished by being put to bed early. 'The moral of that story is that at the end they'll be in bed and not be able to go out and do anything, so it shows that if you do something wrong you'll get punished for it.' These students are analysing the effect of the stories that they read, making comparisons with other texts, relating them to real life and making value judgement on texts ... all through reading comics. This seems to me to be a good reason for keeping some in a book box for private reading. It is of course necessary to allow opportunity for the sort of discussions which brought out those comments to take place, both to appreciate the judgements that they are making and to allow them to gain confidence in their opinions and to validate the decision to read a wide range of different texts.

Another section allied to comics is magazines. It is sometimes quite difficult to be successful with these as they are often ephemeral, particularly those about music or those published weekly or monthly for a very specific audience. However, a colleague recently donated a pile of fishing magazines which have proved very popular with the boys, as do magazines about skateboarding or other extreme sports. All of these can act as tasters to validate the material that boys, in particular, do read and to make reading less distant for them.

Graphic novels

Linked to comics are the more highly developed graphic novels. These are subject to the same objections as comics: impoverished language, violence and an awareness that their themes are not very politically correct. While these criticisms are undoubtedly true of much of the genre, there are some works which have merit and which are of real interest to our audience, so we need to find a place for them in our reading boxes. The techniques used: bubble writing, comic-strip format and a variety of typefaces are all things which young people recognize from advertisements, posters, magazines and leaflets and they will work harder to access more complex information in this format than from a page of plain text. The interaction of text and visuals makes it possible to present more sophisticated language and ideas which might otherwise seem too difficult. Think of *Asterix* or the humour and linguistic complexity of the Church Mice series for younger children.

Stories in which the visual element predominates are often less daunting, an idea which has made the HarperCollins Jets series such a success for younger and less expert readers. Graphic novels are not just for the inexperienced reader though. Philip Pullman's *Spring-heeled Jack* combines pages of text with the usual frames of the comic strip and both are essential to an understanding of the story. The pictures advance the plot with information not found in the text and the illustrations take the place of paragraphs of description.

This adult nature of some graphic novels is also demonstrated in Raymond Briggs' *When the Wind Blows* where the seriousness of the story of the aftermath of a nuclear strike is heightened by the humour of the couple's attempt to comply with the instructions given in the government leaflet. The important effect of this is to tell a familiar story in a fresh and accessible way for a new audience. This is not a comic for children which can be dismissed as sub-standard literature making no demands on its audience because it uses the techniques of comic-strip storytelling.

Poetry

I have talked about the provision of a selection of poetry books in class libraries in Chapter 9, The Reader-Friendly Classroom, but it is worth reiterating here. I accept that it is not encouraging the committed read which a novel provides, but the nature of poetry to provide reading in small doses is often a useful one. For some students the brief nature of the text makes it accessible and far less daunting than the prospect of a wordy book. The covers are often bright and colourful which students like and they have titles which are sometimes funny and attract attention. Many of the poems can be read on different levels so they may well have encountered some texts in primary school. They then feel like old friends. 'I Heard it in the Playground' is always enjoyed as is 'Down Behind the Dustbin' and reminding students, who are reluctant readers, of reading experiences which gave them pleasure helps to change their view of themselves.

Many of the poetry anthologies that are available have poems that will raise a laugh and encourage their readers to share. This sharing of texts which are enjoyed is a valuable part of gaining confidence and pleasure in reading and creating real readers. It also signals to students that we accept that it is not always appropriate for them to read to order. When students forget their books or finish one in the middle of a lesson, something that can be read and enjoyed without committing them for a long period is indispensable in our understanding of reader habits. Finally, poetry can provide important new ways of seeing the world.

Suggestions for poetry books

Gareth Owen & John Bendall-Brunillo	*My Grannie is a Sumo Wrestler*
Allan Ahlberg & Fritz Wegner	*Please Mrs Butler* (Puffin Books)
Alfred Noyes & Charles Keeping	*The Highwayman*
Benjamin Zephaniah	*Funky Chickens* (Puffin Poetry)
Brian Patten	*Gargling with Jelly* (Puffin Books)
Colin McNaughton	*Have You Seen Who's Just Moved in Next Door to Us?*
Gervase Phinn	*The Day Our Teacher Went Batty*
Gez Walsh & Julie Thompson	*The Spot on My Bum: Horrible Poems for Horrible Children*
Iona & Peter Opie	*I Saw Esau*
Kit Wright & P. Simmonds	*Cat Among the Pigeons* (Puffin Books)
Michael Rosen	*Centrally Heated Knickers* (Puffin Poetry)
Roald Dahl & Quentin Blake	*Revolting Rhymes*
T.S. Eliot & Edward Gorey	*Old Possum's Book of Practical Cats*
Ted Hughes & Seamus Heaney	*The Rattle Bag*
Bruce Lansky	*My Dog Ate My Homework*
Gez Walsh	*Parents, Zits and Hairy Bits: The World According to Wilf*
	A Year Full of Poems (OUP)
Andrew Fusek Peters	*Poems with Attitude*
Mick Gowar	*So Far So Good*
Mick Gowar	*Carnival of the Animals*
Adrian Henri	*Spooky Poems*
Sandy Brownjohn	*Both Sides of the Catflap*
James Berry	*When I Dance*
Poems by women poets (Collected by Wendy Cope)	*Is That the New Moon?*
Anecdotal poems (ed. Michael Rosen)	*Action Replay*
(ed. Anne Harvey)	*In Time of War*
A book of story poems (Chosen by Brian Patten)	*Gangsters, Ghosts and Dragonflies*

Poems about people (ed. Anne Harvey)	*Faces in a Crowd*
The Works [Every kind of poem you need for the Literacy hour]	
	(chosen by Paul Cookson)
The Works 3: A Poet a Week	(chosen by Paul Cookson)

Audio books

It is also useful to keep some audio books. Many of us enjoy the process of being read to and audio books can provide access to texts for students who may not be able to read them for themselves. Sometimes they can supplement work on a class reader with a weaker reader being able to keep up with the rest of the class by listening at home. The use of audio books also means students can keep up with some of the current favourite texts in the class and, if the text is unabridged, they can follow as the text is read which will support their own reading development. Listening Books, also known as the National Listening Library (www.listening-books.org.uk), was founded in 1959 with a simple objective: to supply audio books to anyone unable to read in the usual way and they will help to supply books for students with disabilities who cannot access texts in the normal way. This means that blind or partially sighted children can have an alternative to Braille or large-print books and can share texts simultaneously with others by the use of headphones.

The one area I haven't mentioned here is students' own writing. When students write stories they always enjoy swapping them around and reading each other's. If they worked on the drafting process together they like to see what the finished product turned out like and it is good to keep a collection of their stories and poems for private reading sessions. Many students wordprocess work these days, so it is very easy to keep a loose-leaf folder to which you can add throughout the year. As these span the year groups it also gives younger students a sense of what they are aspiring to.

11 Reading plays

Play scripts can be a great way of getting students to read. Choosing a play script as the basis of a scheme of work can actively involve a large number of students. Reading a play is an activity that the majority of students like, particularly if you are careful to find something that they can relate to or find amusing. As students are expected at GCSE to be able to comment on the dramatic structure, devices and stagecraft that playwrights use, reading plays is an important part of their reading in lower school. The nature of a script makes it more accessible to a wide range of students and can provide real encouragement for reluctant readers. The active part taken also encourages greater ownership of a text.

It is easier for some students to see a purpose in reading a play. They can identify with the character that they are reading and many are more ready to discuss motivation when they see themselves as that person. Making inferences can also be made easier by the active nature of the tasks that you can perform when reading plays.

You do have a number of decisions to make when planning how to use a play script. You can put students into small groups to prepare a reading of certain sections of the play which they then read out smoothly. The chance to prepare a reading makes it possible for them to ensure that they know how to pronounce all of their words and to think about what their character is feeling to make sure that the tone of voice is right. A small group of friends will help each other in deciding on interpretation and much useful discussion can take place here. A drama space can be a great help but if you can move chairs in a classroom then it is possible to set up a scene for the action to take place in which each group follows on from the group before. Reading the opening of the text to decide on how to set out a scene gives a purpose, and determining what props will be needed from what actions the characters make keeps the task very specific. You can also develop the drama aspects of this and encourage more polished performances of specific sections of text which have been read and re-read. The repetition of words and phrases which may have initially been beyond the reading level of some students can help to transfer them into their working vocabulary when practising a reading.

Sometimes you can choose to allow students to read a whole play together without presenting it to the rest of the group. Again this has advantages. Students who will not choose to read out in class may happily take a part in a group of their friends. This can work as an alternative to private reading for students who find silent concentration difficult. Allowing a group of friends to read a script together still gives them the reading practice and acknowledges the need to widen the scope of their reading. It allows them to read aloud, and gives them shared pleasure in the reading. Tony Robinson's *Maid Marian and her Merry Men* and Betsy Byars's *Computer Nut* both work well in this context.

Another possibility is to work with students on writing their own play scripts. The Year 8 writing strategy says that students need to 'experiment presenting material in different forms'. This is fun to do with a novel that a class is reading. Students can work in groups to take a section of the novel and to present it as a play script. Once students are familiar with the layout of a play text they can begin to work out what is needed and how to convey description. A useful method is to look at a piece of dialogue:

'Shall we go in?' Sarah whispered.

and to show them how to move the speaker to the beginning, to turn the verb to an adjective and place it as a stage direction.

Sarah: (whispering) Shall we go in?

This means that some very close reading of the text is done with a very specific purpose in mind but the reading is incidental to the creation of the script which they may well later want to perform or record.

Creating a radio play is another way of getting reading done without students realizing. First, you need to spend some time looking at the differences between radio and stage plays. Once these distinctions are understood the task of writing for a radio audience can get underway. This can be a spin-off from genre work where the writing is in play rather than story form. Ghost stories on the radio are usually fun and Microsoft's Creative Writer does have some sound effects which students can add while writing to remind themselves of where they need to put them. Use a wordprocessor and put students in pairs for discussion about appropriate language for different characters and collaboration on plot development. This makes it easy to provide multiple copies for reading and easier for extra characters, not involved in the writing, to read their parts. Recording the play with sound effects is fun and means extra reading practice to ensure a smooth broadcast.

Finally, there is the school production which offers the ultimate reading experience for a number of students. Learning lines involves a different discipline from any other reading but the opportunity to play with alternative ways of speaking and to perform in front of an audience builds confidence in a way that little else can. Interestingly, often students who would struggle to read a novel for pleasure can succeed in learning their lines for a performance.

12 Private reading activities

Reading for pleasure is one strand of what we want our students to do. To do that they also need to be critical readers who have views about what they read. They need to develop strategies to help them make judgements and the suggestions here for activities to complete after reading are ways of helping them. For many students an automatic expectation that they will have to write about what they have been reading as a way of aiding and demonstrating their understanding is enough to put them off. We need to balance that knowledge with our need to know that they have understood and perhaps learned something from what they have read and to help us to move on their reading. If we don't know what effect a particular book has had on them, or how challenging they found it, how can we know what direction to point them in to move them on?

So you want them to respond to what they have read, but not necessarily in writing. The following are some suggestions, written, visual and oral, that you might want to use. Many are useful because recommendations from other students are very important tools in encouraging students when choosing books.

- Having a bulletin board in your classroom where students can put blurbs or recommendations of books that they have enjoyed. You could extend this to show the book of the month, if more than one student has read and enjoyed the same book. I know that a reading tree is a little old-fashioned but Year 7 still like this visual representation. If your pastoral scheme allows time for private reading then using graphs/ tables in tutor rooms to show what students have read can be effective. This gives reading value beyond the work in English.

- Make story tapes of the openings of books that they have particularly enjoyed. They will need to practise their reading first and can include music or sound effects. This is a good collaboration exercise and fulfils literacy strategy objectives for drama where students are expected to 'extend their spoken repertoire by experimenting with language in different roles and dramatic contexts'. These tapes can then be used to stimulate interest in other readers and can be used in private reading sessions. Following the text while a good reader models the reading is also helpful for less able readers. While it couldn't replace a partner in paired reading it can fulfil some of the same objectives.
- Produce a family tree of the relationships in the book. These make good display material in the classroom and again can be a support for less able readers. This, incidentally, can be a good exercise with older students at A-level trying to keep track of relationships in a Victorian novel.
- Imagine that a new film is being made of your book. Design a cinema poster to advertise it.
- For someone who has read a book about teenage life they could identify how the writer has captured the voice of the teenager. Louise Rennison's books about Georgia Nicolson, or *Adrian Mole*, *The Catcher in the Rye* or *Diary of a Teenage Health Freak* would all work well here. Readers could then write an account of an experience in their own lives using the same methods or produce a photo-story using thought bubbles.
- If they have read a story which involves the characters in difficult situations with personal dilemmas they could write a letter to an agony aunt from one of them and also the reply. Many enjoy the chance to say what they think the character should have done in that situation, i.e. how they would have handled it themselves.
- Imagine that a new television series is being made of your book. When a number of students have read the same book, then they could prepare the film trailer for the series or on their own prepare a storyboard for the trailer.
- If the book is about a journey or a quest, then draw a map to show routes taken and show where important events occur.

- When two students have read the same book, write or improvise a scene in which two characters from the book meet at some time in the future and discuss people and events from the past.
- Choose a character from the book and imagine a dream or nightmare that they might have had.
- Ask them to pick out a character from the last two books that they have read who they would like as their friend. They need to justify their decisions and point to events in the book to support their comments.
- Choose a character, who is not the main one, and write diary entries for him/her at important moments in the book or write entries for all the main characters at a particular crisis point in the story.
- Imagine that one of the characters is to be interviewed on television on his/her life and about the events in the book. Write down the questions that might be asked and answer them as if you were the character. This works well if two students have read the same book.
- Choose an exciting or frightening episode from the book and produce a front-page tabloid report on it. Include interviews with witnesses and any rumours as well as a description of the event.
- Imagine that you are going to re-tell the story to a younger audience. Try to make it as exciting or amusing as possible. You may need to have picture prompts to help you.
- Have a small group of students work together to discuss their books. This works well in threes. Groups of four often split into two who do the work and two who discuss their social life. Give them some prompts: Which character would you most (or least) like to be and at which point in the book? Which character are you most like and in which ways are you similar or different? Have you learnt anything from reading this book?
- Look at the opening of the novel and write a short chapter which comes before it. Write an alternative ending for it.
- Run a book programme; video it. You could give them various possible activities to do.
- If the book has plenty of action, write it up as a detective's

case study showing who: main characters, heroes, villains, victims; what happened: when, to whom, how; where: place, country, is the location significant to what happens; why: motives, causes, explanations, evidence; with what result, conclusion?

Book Programme

As a group you are going to produce a magazine programme introducing a number of books. You could:

- dramatize a brief extract to whet an audience's appetite;
- write a mock interview with the author or a character;
- design a TV advert to sell the book;
- create a series of tableaux with voice overs.

- Use the format of the Battle of the Books which the Big Read used and challenge students to defend their book. The rest of the class could then vote on which book they would most like to read. It would be good to show them examples, if you recorded any, to analyse the techniques that the proposers used.
- Use the similar idea of a balloon debate.

The Balloon Debate

If you don't know the idea of a balloon debate, it works like this. A hot-air balloon containing a number of texts is not gaining sufficient height to get over Book Mountain. It is necessary to shed some weight. The texts on board are the last copies in the world and only one of them can remain in the balloon for it to make the climb. Which text is to be kept for future readers? The class is to decide. This can be as big or small a project as you wish. You could set it up with six students who feel passionately about something they have read, while others produce a different response to their reading, or you could do it with a whole class. They need time to prepare their arguments on why their chosen text is special and deserves to be saved. When each person has presented his/her case the rest of the class can vote on which their preferred choice is. There are resource materials which you can download on this from the National Literacy Trust at www.readon.org.uk/tbr.html. When you log on here go to the Secondary Schools Beyond the Big Read section and there are worksheets and a series of lessons related to the aims of the Literacy Strategy to help you to set up a balloon debate.

Many of these activities can be good ways of fulfilling the demands of the Speaking and Listening strands of the Literacy Strategy. For example, let us look at the suggestion of re-telling a story for a younger audience. The Year 8 Teaching Objectives state that pupils should be taught to 'tell a story, recount an experience or develop an idea, choosing and changing the mood, tone and pace of delivery for particular effect'. A story which they have chosen themselves, enjoyed and know well can be a good starting point for the discussion of tone and pace to create involvement and interest.

The balloon debate provides an opportunity to 'make a formal presentation in standard English, using appropriate rhetorical devices' and to 'promote, justify or defend a point of view using supporting evidence, example and illustration which are linked back to the main argument', and for those who are watching and deciding who to vote off, rather like in Big Brother, they will have the chance to 'discuss and evaluate conflicting evidence to arrive at a considered viewpoint'.

The television interview in the role as a character from the book demonstrates their ability to 'answer questions pertinently, drawing on relevant evidence or reasons'.

13 Computers and reading

Computer games

Kids like playing computer games but most parents and teachers would say that they would rather they were reading books. This is particularly true of boys whose parents often complain about the fact that they spend so much time on games. Even when they do read, their tastes are different; girls' reading is often seen as more relevant because it matches the demands of the English curriculum more closely while access to games is usually banned in classrooms. Students who try to play are often banned from use of the computers. Computer games are a controversial medium in today's society and whenever children are involved in violent activities the press trots out all the old arguments about how computer games are sources of mindless violence where children are encouraged to act out violent fantasies or blur the boundaries of reality and fantasy and create non–communicating children who are tied to screens avoiding all human contact. Of course we have met all of these demons of new media many times before whenever any new medium becomes widespread. You only have to think of the way that novel reading was attacked in the nineteenth century for the concerns of the moral weaknesses it promoted, the controversy over comics and television in the twentieth century, and the misgivings about the Internet to see that suspicion of new media is a normal response.

Is it right then to dismiss computer games in this way or do they have any importance in getting students to read? In the June 2004 NATE *English, Drama, Media* magazine, Andrew Burn, Assistant Director of the Centre for the Study of Children, Youth and the Media at the London Institute of Education in an article called 'From *The Tempest* to *Tomb-Raider*', examines the way in which computer games can 'enhance our teaching of grammar, narrative, literature, culture and drama'. Many English teachers worry, like parents, that these games don't fit in with accepted literary canon and are suspect in the study of English. They have 'flat' characters and their lives are punctuated only by physical challenges, usually fighting. They show no sign of growing or learning from their experiences and games end with them glorying in their success at coming through rather than reflecting on what they have learned. Andrew Burn suggests that it is inadequate to criticize role-playing games on the basis of characters who show no sign of development in response to their experiences. He argues that some games reflect similar character-istics to some heroic literature where the actions undertaken by the central character are central to the story and character development is minimal. To see what he means, you only have to think of the popular Greek myths where Jason's adventures in acquiring the Golden Fleece show his heroic actions against seemingly insurmountable odds and *Alice in Wonderland* where the surreal puzzle element is the attraction of the story and Alice's own ability to solve puzzles or circumvent them is what keeps people reading. Readers aren't interested in whether Jason has grown in character by the end of the story, only that he has managed to resist the lure of the sirens or escaped the Clashing Rocks; they don't care whether Alice understands herself better, only that she finds her way back out of the rabbit hole. Playing a character in *Baldur's Gate* creates that same need to solve physical problems with any additional magical help you can get and success is the only criterion that matters. The help given in the way of additional qualities earned through actions is also closely reflected in literature. In *The Lord of the Rings* Frodo has help from the elves in the form of energy-restoring lembas-cake as his health fails near the end of his quest, and he wears his elvish chain mail for protection.

So, rather than dismiss these games as a waste of time we need to try to use them to win interest back into novel reading as perhaps a complement, rather than seeing games and reading as mutually exclusive activities. This is where you need to keep the dialogue flowing between you and your students. Ask them to explain what they have to do in their favourite games and in many cases you will find that there is a quest as their central idea with characters who have magical or exceptional powers and qualities. It is quite possible that much of the development of current fantasy novels is in response to the success of game playing where the quest or journey through inhospitable territory is familiar ground for young players. This is a very useful way in for teachers faced with students who would rather play games than read. Here are a few suggestions to start to put to game-playing students:

Books related to fantasy quests

The Lord of the Rings	J. R. R. Tolkien (quest, fantasy creatures, battles, unusual weapons)
Across the Nightingale Floor	Lian Hearn (medieval Japanese setting, swords, unusual challenges, battles)
The Wind Singer	William Nicholson (fantasy world, unusual transport, quest to find voice to free the people)
Sabriel	Garth Nix (quest to learn role of Abhorson, necromancer. Magical equipment, unknown powers)
Mortal Engines	Philip Reeve (world regressed after war, loss of technology, so ancient weapons and society)
Northern Lights	Philip Pullman (unusual creatures, weapons, quest to save victims)
The Shadow of the Minotaur	Alan Gibbons (this is even more closely linked in that Phoenix's father creates a virtual reality suit which allows the game player to be inside the game. It all becomes a little too real and Phoenix becomes Theseus and various Greek heroes)

Of course, when you look at these titles it is not true to say that they fit into the category of books where character development is minimal and physical challenge is all important. No one who has read Philip Pullman could fail to be involved with the complexity of Lyra's life and growth into adulthood.

They can however, be useful ways into texts. The final book on the list is particularly interesting because game players will feel very much at home in the world that it inhabits. The book regularly uses the terminology of game-playing when Phoenix, the central character, is drawn into the game. This is typically second-person where the reader becomes the protagonist and is directly addressed, as in the following introduction to the game Astonia: 'Welcome stranger to the dangerous lands of Astonia. Great perils await thee on thy travels here. May thy blade be swift and thy magic superior'. Not only is the terminology of game-playing here but the book follows the pattern of a game with different levels being reached by the player who has yet more difficult challenges to face. As the hero of the game is also a real character we are aware of his emotional life too. His fear and uncertainty at his ability to face up to the challenge gives the book depth and reality to the character:

> Taking a deep, shuddering breath he finally managed to pass the string through the hatch and secure it to one of the little bars in the opening. Weighing the sword uncertainly in his hand and letting the string play out behind him, he took his first faltering steps down the dark passageway.

Normally the game player's breath is not 'shuddering' as he negotiates a problem and his sword won't hang 'uncertainly' in his hand, but students will recognize the need to move forwards down a 'dark passageway'. This recognition could bring fiction closer to the sort of entertainment usually enjoyed by boys and allow them to see that there is enjoyment to be gained here. It could also make fiction less threatening and reassuringly familiar.

Another possibility for linking written texts to computer games is the Fighting Fantasy series by Steve Jackson and Ian Livingstone which seems to be having a comeback since its origins in the early 1980s. The books are again second-person texts which put the reader directly into the position of the central character and present a narrative which is determined by the choices that are made. For example:

> You are standing on a deserted heath with a storm about to break over you. To the east is a ramshackle building without a

glimmer of light breaking through the gloom over it. To the North is a wide rushing river. . . . Do you go east, west, north or south?

Again student game players will recognize the choices that they have to make and know that the responsibility for the way that the narrative turns out is theirs. Obviously, without the graphics which accompany games these may seem very tame, but the familiarity can be enough to get some boys into books and we always have some available in book boxes. Boys often respond more readily to a task whose purpose is clear to them and writing a comparison between one of these books and games that they play, rather than the usual review, reaps rewards.

There is also scope here for detailed analytical work on the narrative structures involved in games and comparative work on game versions of popular pieces of literature like Harry Potter and *The Lord of the Rings*.

Using the Internet for reading–related research

So far I have looked at how computers and specifically games can link to the reading of fiction, but there is a whole area of reading around fiction which can be useful in encouraging students to read. The Internet provides a wealth of opportunities for background research on writers and books which can be used to stimulate interest and sometimes to enter into dialogues with writers. As all current thinking shows that it is boys who are the most reluctant readers some of the suggestions are designed with boys in mind but it is important to be careful not to disadvantage girls in the process. Any scheme to encourage students to read more and to broaden the scope of their reading must work equally with girls as well. Building on students' interest in popular culture and the media is equally attractive to both sexes.

Let's look now at some suggestions where you can use the information about writers that is available on the Internet. The obvious one is to research the background of a particular author. It is possible to find information about all of the current popular authors on a variety of user-friendly websites, some more exciting than others. J. K. Rowling's, for example, at www.jkrowling.com/ reflects the style of the Harry Potter books. The front page is a collage of items; she says it's her desk, tidied especially for the occasion, and moving the cursor provides access to News, Rumours, Fan Sites, a scrapbook, a biography, Wizard of the Month, Extra Stuff, Frequently Asked Questions and Links. The last provides access to the Warner Brothers' Harry Potter movie website. Her website is attractive, colourful and very child-friendly in its style as well as being informative.

Needless to say, there are a number of websites which feature popular writers like Jacqueline Wilson, for example: this one from the BBC, www.bbc.co.uk/arts/books/author/wilson/. This provides a biography and interview with her but also has a link to the Tracey Beaker website on CBBC which is aimed for an audience of 7- to 11-year-olds but will be popular with her fans. It gives games to play and quizzes, all based around the Tracey Beaker stories.

Another interesting one for Jacqueline Wilson is at www.mystworld.com/youngwriter/authors/jacqwilson.html. This is an in-depth interview with her by student readers and covers many of the questions that are always asked of writers by their readers as well as some more unusual ones. The home website for Young Writers at: www.mystworld.com/youngwriter/ index.html has a series of interviews which you could use as material for research. Here is a selection from that list:

- Michelle Magorian
- Gillian Cross
- David Almond
- Carol Ann Duffy
- Peter Dickinson
- Philip Pullman
- Kit Wright
- Michael Morpurgo
- Malorie Blackman
- Robert Swindells
- Anne Fine
- Brian Jacques
- Benjamin Zephaniah
- Terry Pratchett

The final Jacqueline Wilson website to recommend is that of her publishers, Random House. Use www.kidsatrandomhouse.co.uk/ jacquelinewilson/. This also provides biographical information in the form of '50 questions you have always wanted to ask' and has a complete list of her books as well as having other useful links like showing where Jacqueline Wilson is doing book signings, where the latest play is being shown and previews of the newest book. Finally, there are quite lengthy extracts with enough to really whet the appetite for those who may not have read any of her books before.

Two websites with more appeal for boys are those of Darren Shan and Garth Nix. Shan's stories about the half-vampire are popular and his website is visually attractive with the usual background information as well as details of how to contact him and to join the mailing list (www.darrenshan.com/). It also has a series of links, most of which are very personal interests, but includes the link to another well-liked writer in the form of Eoin Colfer: www.homepage.eircom.net/~eoincolfer65/. The music will annoy you but again there are links to Colfer's biography, extracts and reviews of the books and some fun in the form of a code-breaking exercise.

Some of the Garth Nix websites are rather more interesting. The HarperCollins site, www.garthnix.co.uk, is good as it involves a game as well as information about the author. There are pictures and explanations of important ingredients of the books, like *Necromancer Bells* and *Charter Marks*, and a map of the Old Kingdom. The following homepage for Nix is a series of links to other sections and includes a very early choose your own adventure game by Nix which some may enjoy playing: eidolon.net/ homesite.html?author=garthnix. Finally, this American website also has some interesting information: www.abhorsentrilogy.com/ abhorsen.html.

The best website on Philip Pullman seems to be: www.bridgetothestars.net/. It has access to all the usual biographical material, but also has links to other information that fans will find interesting. For example, at the moment there is discussion of the proposed movie of *His Dark Materials* and who will direct it and links to read about the stage version. There are also biographies of the major characters which would be useful to anyone going to see the play who hasn't read the book for some time.

Baudelaire family fans can find Lemony Snicket's website at www.lemonysnicket.com/. This is Daniel Handler's homepage and is written in keeping with the pessimism of the books. Fans will find it amusing but it may be off-putting for those who haven't actually enjoyed the books. It does have a simple racing game and trailers from the film.

Most writers now have a homepage with their information, all of which can be useful when setting up a research task.

List of useful author websites

Michael Morpurgo:	www.childrenslaureate.org/index.htm
Malorie Blackman:	www.malorieblackman.co.uk/pages/ games.html
Alan Gibbons:	www.alangibbons.com/
Anne Fine:	www.annefine.co.uk
Anthony Horowitz:	wwwchannel4.com/learning/microsites/B/ bookbox/authors/horowitz/index1.htm
Terry Pratchett:	www.turtlesalltheway.com/ (under construction at time of writing) www.terrypratchettbooks.com/
Louise Rennison	www.teenreads.com/authors/au-rennison-louise
David Almond	www.davidalmond.com/
R. L. Stine	www.scholastic.com/goosebumps/books/ stine/ www.thenightmareroom.com/ www.sharyn.org/authors.html

This website is an extensive collection of author websites. You should be able to find anyone you want here.

How you create the research project depends very much on the computer access at your school. If your students have dedicated ICT lessons where they are taught how to use the Internet and how to judge the usefulness of a website then you can go straight into research. If not you will need to do some groundwork with them about how to choose and use websites. While I have made a few suggestions to get things started, you will need to look at the websites yourself to ensure that the information that you want students to find is accessible. The following checklist might be useful to you.

- Is the main purpose of the website clear and obvious without too many confusing options? Does the homepage show you that you will be able to find the information that you want?
- Is the design clear enough? Is the typeface readable? Some of the websites that I have identified are related to the writer's genre, so Garth Nix's is quite dark on first entry.
- Is the 'character' of the website friendly and welcoming, challenging and exciting?
- Is the age group of the website clear? Is the language appropriate for the target age group?
- Is the website easy to navigate? Is it easy to return to the homepage?
- Is it possible to contribute to the website? What incentive is there for students to do this?

The project I set students is to create author posters. They should be colourful, clear and informative and may be done by hand or computer. We then laminate them and use them for display around the school. The posters should include:

1. A factfile with basic information about the author: photograph, name, age, where he/she lives, family, past jobs, own reading likes/dislikes.
2. List of books by this author.
3. An extract from one of the books.
4. A review of one or two books.
5. Any advice given to prospective writers.
6. Some indication of genre in the pictures. These could be copies of front covers or own drawings for the book.

These are the basics but the students can choose any additional information that they want to include.

In the past, students have presented the information that they have found in a PowerPoint presentation and these can be put on the school's Intranet for access by anyone.

Reading groups on the Internet

The Internet is also very useful for finding other readers and recommendations of what to read next, both for teachers and students. There are a number of websites which offer readers the chance to come together to talk about their reading and to recommend books to each other. The first is a website at www.4ureaders.net. This is aimed at early teens and is separated into sections: The Lads, Girls with Attitude, and e-claire. Each section includes suggestions of book titles both for and from the target audience but includes other activities as well, for example game reviews in the Lads section. The top five for boys (I found it interesting that they were in a list of best books. It reminded me of *High Fidelity* and the need to make lists) were:

- *Martyn Pig* by Kevin Brooks
- *Cirque Du Freak* by Darren Shan
- *Hacker* by Malorie Blackman
- *Grass* by C. Z. Nightingale
- *Toad Rage* by Morris Gleizman

The Girls with Attitude section just included a number of titles without any hierarchy. The first ones on the list were:

- *Coraline* by Neil Gaiman
- *Private Peaceful* by Michael Morpurgo
- *Outcast of Redwall* by Brian Jacques
- *A Gathering Light* by Jennifer Donnelly
- *Noughts and Crosses* by Malorie Blackman

Although the site is separated by gender for entry and the homepage is very gender-specific, it is interesting that the booklists read like teacher recommendations which are read by either sex.

There is also a chance to send in book reviews, stories and poems for others to access on the website, and there is something called Book Brother. Here blurbs of two books from a selection are given and readers are invited to vote for the next book to be thrown out. It also has a Safe Surfing section with a reminder for students on how to keep themselves safe in chatrooms.

www.word-of-mouth.org.uk works on a similar principle of

sharing good ideas with other readers, but it is aimed at a more adult audience, although reviews of some children's fiction are posted, some by young people and some by adults. Older, good readers would find something here to try and the reviews are brief and personal, an incentive to write and send in their own. The sections are themed or grouped: 'BUZZ, the book everyone enjoys talking about. CHALLENGE, incredibly tough reads – were they really worth it? INDULGENCE, books read purely for enjoyment. Share your favourite books here'.

My final three websites might be more useful for staff and could be made available on an Intranet for them. They are:

- www.the-zone.org.uk which is the website of the Lincolnshire Library Service;
- askchris.essexcc.gov.uk/adult/welcome.asp is the Essex Library service;
- www.readerville.com is an American website dedicated to 'the social life of the mind'.

If you haven't heard of www.bookcrossing.com it might be worth running a similar scheme in your school. I haven't tried it yet, but I'm tempted.

It is impossible to cover the wealth of material about books which can be found online; some of my suggestions here may be gone by the time this book comes out, however there are websites which will not disappear that you can tap into at any time.

- The Carnegie website will support you in the shadowing scheme: www.carnegiegreenaway.org.uk/.
- www.achuka.co.uk/ will you give a world of information on writers and books as well as very useful links to other related websites.
- www.booktrust.org.uk/.
- www.seemore.mi.org/booklists/. This is probably the most comprehensive booklist I know. It covers books in any genre you could wish to find and even includes a 'if you liked this, try this' section.
- www.worldbookdayfestival.com/2004/. This website is worth a look even if it is not near the date because there

are accessible archives of the previous Days with video clips of writers and teenagers talking about their appeal.

www.englishonline.co.uk/ is one more website worth knowing about. Schools can buy into it with e-learning credits and gain access for whole departments and students. There are a number of goodies for teachers, including lesson plans and revision sessions for students on the most popular GCSE texts, but the area I want to talk about here concerns writers. Typing writers@actis.co.uk will take you to a section where writers challenge young people to develop an idea in relation to an extract from their own writing. The writers involved are: Nigel Hinton, Trevor Millum, Elizabeth Laird, Neil Arksey, Terence Blacker and Keith Gray and the suggestions range from writing from the second character in the extract's point of view through poetry, in the form of spells, to opening on a moment of sporting high drama. When the scheme was first started the best pieces were posted on the website with comment from the writers involved and these can still be read there. At the time of writing Tom Rank at Actis says that the best student pieces will still be posted on the website. This would make a useful challenge for Years 7 or 8 who could work collaboratively on a piece of their choice, with possible access to a wide audience, and would tap into student interest in working with modern media.

14 The shared class reader

The Literacy Hour uses sections of texts to create 'fluent and independent readers' who can be 'critical and discriminating in response to a wide range of printed and critical texts'. This has ensured that some students can read closely for meaning and have been introduced to a variety of genres. I feel that we do students a disservice if we do not also introduce them to the experience of sharing whole books with other students. There are a number of children who do not have reading role models at home and, if we do not read novels with them in class, will never choose to do so for themselves.

Sharing stories is an old tradition. Oral storytellers often had a revered position in societies across the world. Great status was accorded to the person who could bring the world to life through words and remind the group of their place in their world and how it began. The experience of enjoying a shared book is important for students:

- it can create a shared identity;
- they can make judgements which they can validate against others;
- they can recognize differing ways of reading;
- they can hear good reading modelled both by the teacher and by students in the group;
- they can experience the pleasure of shared laughter and intense excitement in cliffhanging episodes;
- and they can share the discussion of predicting what will happen.

In the same way that we take pleasure in the turn of a phrase, the surprising end of a short story or the subtlety of the organization of a novel as individual readers, that enjoyment can be heightened by sharing it with others. All teachers of literature will have had those moments when the class take a collective breath at the awfulness of the rat catcher's behaviour in the Roald Dahl story unfolding before them or share the injustice of Callum's hanging in *Noughts and Crosses*.

A well-chosen class reader can also stimulate discussion about issues which engage young teenagers and introduce topics which will excite their interest in the world around them. When novels deal with ideas about 'freedom', 'injustice', 'homelessness', 'prejudice' and 'family relationships' we must not miss these chances to introduce students to respect and enjoy the similarities and differences in the range of views heard in the classroom.

Having said that, it is important to choose a book for the quality of its writing rather than just for the issues it raises. Books designed to make it easier to teach PSHE rarely satisfy in their content. Students recognize when they are being patronized and dislike the overt messages given. For example: bullying is an issue rarely far from the agenda for schools. It is possible to find any number of books which will give the message that it is wrong to do it. Some will show the bully as victim too and most show a satisfactory resolution for the victim, but young people know that bullying continues despite efforts to stop it. More satisfying are those novels in which bullying happens but the characterization is more important, as in Alan Gibbons's *The Edge* where racism and the problems of troubled marriages are fundamental to the story. Anne Fine's *The Tulip Touch* caused controversy when it came out, stimulated she said, by the Jamie Bulger killing. Here the relationship between two young girls is explored delicately, demonstrating the increasing violence with which one of them influences those around her. Students find echoes of themselves or their own behaviour in both characters and it allows them to judge the consequences of certain actions while remaining distanced from them. It is a disturbing book, but there is room within our classrooms for literature that disturbs and perhaps shocks. Students hear the news and read newspapers which reflect the society in which we live and can recognize the reality of narrative situations.

Deconstructing front covers before studying a book in class can be fun as well as fulfilling the Literary Strategy. It draws in students, who make their own suggestions and predictions before reading. Listening to the suggestions of others helps them to crystallize their own ideas and gives readers a platform to make their own judgements as they share the text. Reading for meaning requires students to 'review their developing skills as active, critical readers' and to make predictions about texts. Recognizing genre conventions in visual images and then tracing their appearance in the actual text can lead to sophisticated judgements and more critically literate students. It can also generate discussion about the psychology of covers and the role of reading in society. Students are often intrigued by a publisher's decision to produce an adult and a child version of the same text. Having worked on the cover before reading also allows decisions to be made after reading, on producing alternatives.

This is not the place to provide suggestions on what to do when reading specific novels in class; you can get work schemes on particular texts from a wide variety of sources, but there are some general comments which I think are worth making. Sometimes you may want to read a novel alongside a scheme of work without it being the major focus of writing. For example, we use a scheme of work on *A Midsummer Night's Dream* in Year 8 and this is often a good place to read *King of Shadows* by Susan Cooper. The main focus is the work on the Shakespeare play, but the time-slip story involving a boy playing Puck at the Globe today and in Shakespeare's time lends itself well to background reading. You can choose to use the book in different ways. You may decide that the students will keep a reading journal as they progress through the book. Reading journals are a good way to keep a personal record of their responses to what happens. They can create involvement in the characters and allow speculation about what is happening. Here are some suggestions to give to students about what to put in a reading journal.

Reading Journals

- If you have spent time looking at the front cover, then the first entry gives their predictions both of the genre and the possible plot based upon their observations.

- Read the first chapter and record feelings about the main characters and the situation they find themselves in. Keep commenting on how the story makes you feel throughout the book, charting any changes. Make sure you explain why you feel differently.
- Try to record the emotions created as you go through the book. Did any of the characters make you angry at their behaviour, feel sorry for them, laugh at them?
- Are there any aspects of the book that remind you of yourself or anyone you know? Does it seem true to life in the way that it deals with that experience?
- Are there any of the characters that you would like to be or have as your friend?
- Is everything in the book straightforward and easy to understand or are there difficulties and confusions?
- Are any of the ideas in the book new to you? Do they make you stop and think or make you ask questions?
- Is the language easy to understand? Were there any sections that really made an impression on you? Copy out any lines that you really liked into your reading journal.
- Has reading this book changed you at all? Have you learned anything about the world or yourself that you didn't know before?
- Would you read any more books by this author or have you already read any? Why or why not?

Obviously you can set this up with the suggestions for students before you begin reading the book and they can write their comments as you finish reading a section in class or they can have ten minutes at the beginning of lessons to write. This can help to create an orderly and productive start as students know that they have work to do immediately they come in. Although this may seem that students are not sharing the text with the benefits noted at the opening of this section, when the journals are finished students can draw on their comments to open up discussion on the effects that the book had on them. Of course you may choose for them not to write their journal entries until you have discussed the section that you have just read.

I like to set up reading journals when I am reading a new text that we have just bought with a class. Sometimes I read the text very quickly with them setting the journal comments for homework. I tell the class that I am using them as an experiment and that I want to know what the good and bad points about this text are. They then use their journals to write a critique on using that particular text for me and make suggestions of the activities they would like to do with it if we were studying it.

Another area to think about when sharing a text with a class is how to read it. Modelling good reading for students is a useful practice and can be done by you or by good readers in the class. We all know how painful it is, both for the readers themselves and for the rest of the class, when all students take it in turns to read so we need to find ways to make it possible for all readers to have a turn but without embarrassment. Some of these have worked:

- Read around the class, a paragraph each, but allow anyone to signal, we use a knock, if they don't wish to read at this point. This often allows time for weaker readers to learn pronunciations of words which figure regularly but that they didn't know. They can also see how long the paragraph is that they will have to read and can choose.
- Begin reading yourself and model the length you might expect someone to read. When you stop, anyone who wants to read can take over for a while. They can choose how much to read but you can set a limit on how long they can read if you want to. This way the reading flows uninterrupted by you choosing who is to go next.
- If the book, or the section that you are reading, includes a lot of dialogue then assign parts. This can be quite difficult as the speaker is not always given, only understood. Students have to be very aware and stay focused when reading in this way. I begin by reading the narrative sections myself but once they understand the principle I choose good volunteers to read alternate pages each. An incidental spin-off of this is to reinforce the process of setting out speech.
- If students take the book home you can assign sections to

individual students so that they can practise at home. For many it is the initial sight reading that provides the problem, not actually knowing and understanding the words. Practice improves their confidence and puts them level with others in the group.

Part Three

Reading into Writing

15 Reading and writing in genres

Amy Tan's autobiographical pieces *The Opposite of Fate* describe how she began to write. As a child she loved fairy tales with a taste for the grotesque and was awed by the amazingly limitless ways in which lives could be presented and changed in stories. However, a literature degree and a very didactic professor turned her off reading and for a number of years she read few novels. It was not until she began to write short stories for herself that she began to devour books again as she had as a child. The destructive way she had viewed literature as a student, who did not always agree with the ideas of her professors, dissipated as she read more writers with whose sensitivities she identified. She shows that the fascination with understanding and empathizing with characters and ideas is a strong incentive for creating her own. We recognize this link also with students when we ask them to write. If the subject matter is something they know, feel confident and empathize with, the writing is more assured. This was brought home to me when moderating GCSE folders of two top sets this year: one group had written stories which continued from first lines they were given; the second group wrote an extra scene from *Of Mice and Men*. While the first group wrote quite accomplished and well-developed pieces of narrative, the second group showed remarkable sensitivity and were clearly immersed in Steinbeck's world, mirroring his concerns and sympathies.

It is also true that students who read avidly usually write more complex and developed stories than those who don't, but this does not mean that this is always the case. Just because students do not read does not mean that they are unfamiliar with stories. Most of them watch television regularly, rent films or visit the cinema and they may have a clear understanding of some of the different techniques used to move a narrative on. As teachers we can take advantage of this often sophisticated understanding to help both their reading and writing development.

One way to do this is with a genre project where skills of close reading, interpretation and understanding of literary conventions are closely interwoven with the ability to plan effectively, establish the tone and experiment with conventions; all requirements of the Literacy Strategy. Using a project based around a particular genre or choice of genres involves students in making decisions about their reading and gives greater autonomy in the work that they do. As they become the experts it increases confidence and encourages the development of independent work on texts.

Here's how it worked for me. I tend to work on this project with a Year 8 group at the beginning of the Spring term, before the interest in books begins to wane seriously for some readers. We begin focusing on the genre of crime fiction, mainly because even non-readers can be involved from their watching of film and television. The group brainstorm the characteristics of that genre and as a class we then categorize these into characters, plots, methods, settings and atmosphere. Students are often very knowledgeable about these and the confidence gained from bringing sure knowledge to the discussion is helpful to the less assured readers. These are some of the characteristics they came up with.

Characters

- Detective always bright, often misunderstood or uncon-ventional and unusual in some way.
- Sidekick not as clever, taken in by red herrings, useful to have things explained to.
- Victim/s often women or vulnerable or unpleasant, so seem to deserve what they get.

Plots

- Murders for personal gain, revenge, enjoyment (I did wonder what this one had been watching).

- Starting with murder and working out killer; audience don't know until the end.
- Starting with the killer and watching the detectives catch up with him/her.
- Robberies or scams for money.

Ideas

- Interesting weapons.
- Red herrings.
- Alibis often false or misleading.

Settings

- Often domestic.
- Often big city.
- Often car chases.
- Someone who had recently watched an Agatha Christie film talked about limited places where all suspects are kept together.

Atmosphere

- Fear in the lead up to murders or crimes being committed.
- Tension as the detectives get closer.
- Anticipation of further crimes when the detectives seem to be getting nowhere.

We then discuss the various genres of books that they know and like to read. The categorization of books in the school library is very helpful to them here. Finally, each student chooses a genre that they would like to work on. This enables us to make up working groups. Of course there is the question of what to do with students who say that they don't read anything, have no idea about the specific characteristics and whose faces blanch at the thought of reading a whole book. Often there is a student who is interested in drawing among this group, or at least I always hope that there is, and we look at the possibility of a group working on graphic novels or comics. Their brief will still be the same.

Regular enthusiasms for all students are fantasy and horror which is useful as it means that we can have some mixed groups. Chick Lit, with writers like Louise Rennison and the Ally's World series, is also becoming very popular. It is interesting, though, that some students choose to work in a genre that they don't know well. There is also usually a group who like to read what they call 'real-life' stories. The next task is for each group to prepare a list of characteristics like the ones shown above. The group then reports back to the rest of the class on their findings and the lists of characteristics are amended after open discussion. There is often lively argument about the specific features in their chosen genre and the group with their 'real-life' stories usually find themselves talking about issues or problems to be faced rather than the stereotypes of characters like some that we found in the crime genre.

Preparation for this project needs to involve your library or resource centre which provides a selection of texts within the specific genres from which each student chooses a book. I have been lucky enough to be involved in the buying of new texts and this way my students had access to all the new texts that we had chosen as they came in. The choice of book is made in collaboration with their group so that a spread of texts and writers within the genre are chosen. In one very mixed-ability group working on horror, there was a student reading Stephen King with others reading *Point Horror*, *Goosebumps*, Darren Shan and Chris Westwood. This allowed a group of friends with very different reading abilities to work together.

The first reading is set for homework and each student sets themselves a target. This is an opportunity to involve parents and I often inform them that homework will be reading for a couple of weeks to enable the students to finish their books. Parents sign off the number of pages read on the reading log and many end up reading the books themselves. The students have a specific series of tasks while reading. Within their group they have to research all the characteristics that they have described in their list but they can decide how to do that. Sometimes they all try to deal with everything but sometimes they choose to split the areas up between them.˙ This is an advantage for those who have chosen a long book or those who don't read much and again is an advantage for very mixed-ability groups.

I ask all students to keep a reading log of their particular text so that they have a record of their findings for discussion with their groups. In their logs they need to collect examples of text which demonstrate the characteristics that they have found. The specifically analytical nature of this task with a definite number of examples to find is often an advantage with boys who, research has shown, prefer tightly drawn tasks rather than open-ended empathy questions.

Tasks like this, identifying small sections of text, also provide a good opportunity for me to work with small groups on guided reading. First, I bring together all the students who are working on characterization, as some idea of the central character usually appears fairly quickly. Each gives me their example and I put them onto OHT sheets. This allows us to deal with each text and to share observations. Each student can mark up the OHT on their own text as the discussion takes place ready to take back to their group. We work on understanding how readers respond to texts, looking closely at specific techniques liking 'showing not telling' and using inferences and predictions. When we have looked at all the examples, those in the guided group become the experts and report back to their groups on what they have found. The students then write up their observations in their logs for their final report. Each section of the characteristics is dealt with in the same way and each student gets their chance to be the expert in their field. This use of guided reading targets a mixed-ability group with the more able modelling for the weaker students. It also ensures that the rest of the class can get on with the purposeful activities they have already got set out for them.

The group need to organize their reading at home as they go along to make sure that they all finish at the same time. Once the books are finished the groups prepare a brief presentation of their findings which need to include: a brief summary of the story without of course giving away the end; an analysis of how far their chosen stories related to the characteristics of their list; and a reading of some examples from their stories of how these characteristics were demonstrated. This also provides an opportunity for them to show off their computer skills and some of the groups present their findings as a PowerPoint presentation. In the final analysis they sometimes find that they need to make changes to the initial list of characteristics that they have put down as they were insufficiently detailed or as further more subtle characteristics were found.

Of course, it is possible to stop there and just use this as a reading exercise providing the chance to develop independent reading proficiency and specific Speaking and Listening skills in 'formal and collaborative presentation'. However, Peter Traves, Corporate Director for Education and Lifelong Learning in Staffordshire County Council, in 'Reading: the entitlement to be properly literate', puts forward 15 assertions for the concept of 'entitlement' to literacy. He says that, 'children should engage in activities which encourage them to see themselves as producers of texts to be read by themselves and others. Writing and reading are inextricably bound together'. The students know that the reading that they have carried out is legitimate and valued and many of the group are eager to legitimize their writing in the same way, so this is why the next important stage comes with writing. They now have at their fingertips a useful set of guidelines for anyone choosing to write in their chosen genre; they also have annotated examples of how these characteristics are put into practice and, in their discussions to prepare the presentations, they have heard at least three or four different stories. This gives them a similar degree of expertise as the GCSE students writing extra chapters for a text they knew well.

If there are students studying graphic novels the guided 'reading' questions will still look for the same features but here their understanding of visual literacy is brought into play. They look at colour, the use of close-up or long-distance shots and using half-shots to keep the reader guessing at what will come next. Atmosphere in a graphic horror story is created through techniques that they can easily grasp and make explicit in their explanations for others.

Their brief now is to write a story and they have a choice. Some decide to write on their own, while others collaborate. As this is a big piece of work, and I want to use it for assessment, the collaboration cannot be in the actual writing, so if they want to work together, then as a group they decide on the outline of the story and they split it into sections for each one to write. This makes for very interesting discussions about names and exact settings and any details which run throughout the story. As Traves suggests, they read each other's work at regular intervals suggesting changes and supporting achievements. They apply the same standards to their own writing as they identified in the authors that they read and can be quite ruthless with each other in insisting upon revisions of the individual sections of texts to match the rest of the stories.

Those working on graphics have a harder job to make the characters similar when different people are working on sections of the story, but students are endlessly inventive and I have had groups where the characters are drawn by one student and the backgrounds by another, while a third writes the text under the pictures and for the bubbles. Difficult to put an NC level on this but very popular reading for the rest of the class!

The students are very aware of their audiences for these stories. My 'need' to put levels on the stories is less important to them than the way that readers in their own peer group will receive them. Most of them present a typed script with a well-designed front cover, a blurb and the critics' comments on the front. It's great to see so many medal winners among them! The rest of the group obviously enjoy reading each other's stories and these become a useful addition to the class book box. Even the more disaffected readers are encouraged to read whole stories knowing their own contribution. They enjoy seeing how their section fits into the whole.

16 Writing for younger audiences

Sometimes we find that we have to get at reading by the back door when the front door is not only shut but bolted. Students who don't usually read anything unless forced, and certainly not for pleasure, provide the greatest problem. For many of these the antipathy to reading is because their experience of it is threatening as it is always associated with failure. They didn't have the satisfaction of moving up the reading scheme books at the same pace as their peers and could not join in the enthusiasm generated by the discussions of the more challenging and interesting stories which the higher levels were perceived to be involved in. This does of course raise the issue of the use of reading schemes versus real books but perhaps this is not really the place for this discussion. When we talk to students about their experience of learning to read, many cite the satisfaction, while others say they stopped bothering when they couldn't keep up. One boy once told me that he used to cheat. He would tell the teacher that he had completed a level and so was allowed to move on to the space stories that were in fact still beyond him. He was frustrated by not being able to read them although he wanted to, and when he stopped bothering it wasn't noticed.

Many of these students will not become readers for pleasure but sometimes it is possible to set up situations which challenge their perception that reading is not for them. One activity that helped persuade some students back into reading was to write books for younger audiences. Although the Literacy Strategy and the changes in GCSE perhaps make this more difficult to fit in, it is a useful way of both helping reluctant readers at the secondary stage and providing a paired reading activity for younger children.

This activity can work in a number of ways, so let's look at some possibilities. I liked doing it with a Year 10 Foundation group who in our school only enter English language at GCSE. Their target group was a Year 1 class in one of our feeder primaries. I keep a selection of picture books for young readers in my classroom and Year 10 and I spent some time looking at these. This allowed some students to reminisce about their own reading experience, for others to meet old friends and for yet another group to discover the pleasure of intertextuality with *The Jolly Postman*. The reading was easy for them, so there was no sense of failure but, because they had a very specific purpose in reading the books, it was not seen as patronizing. When they had read a selection of them they were allowed to choose which book they would take to the primary school. They were told that they would be reading the book to a pair of children in the class so there was a real incentive to practise and perfect their reading.

I always read *Don't go near the water, Shirley* to them to demonstrate the importance of the pictures in the book. It's great fun. Mum and Dad sit on the beach and the text only consists of the comments they make to Shirley, while the pictures show Shirley and her dog having adventures on a pirate ship culminating with being made to walk the plank. We discussed the importance of the pictures and made suggestions of how a reader can focus on them as well as the words. Obviously, there were usually some of the group who babysat or who had younger brothers or sisters who they read to, so were used to the way that young children like to hear the text in conjunction with the pictures. This was always helpful because it put students, who were used to failure, in the position of experts in this situation and their advice was always well received. Because the focus was on getting it right for the younger ones, there was no problem for my students in asking for the pronunciation of words which they were unsure of and they showed great determination to get it right.

The second part of the task was the writing aspect. After they had read the stories, they were going to talk to the younger ones about the sort of stories they liked and then come back to school to write one for them. We were using the idea of 'me' stories which involve a specific child and the names of people they know. They needed to find out certain details about their audience: names, ages, pets and favourite activities which they were then going to use in the stories they wrote.

The visit to the primary school is always great fun. Our students may have attended it themselves and many of them hadn't been back since they left at age 11. Some were even taught by the same teacher whose class we were visiting so found the whole experience rather strange. The pairings work well and it is good to see sometimes difficult boys taking great care to read well and with expression for the younger ones as well as balancing precariously on chairs which are far too small for them.

When we come back to class there is usually a real buzz about the stories that they are going to write. They know that they need to keep them fairly simple so there is not the usual fear about having to write a long piece. They have learned a great deal about their target audience and with very specific children in mind it is easier to write. If numbers allow, and the work is not for coursework folders, they work in pairs so they devise the story together and include illustrations and an eye-catching front cover.

A great deal of reading goes on in the classroom during the writing of the stories. The most frequent question is 'Do you think they'll understand ... ?' and a word which they think is difficult is explored and decisions made about appropriateness. When the stories are complete they first read them to each other before the final version is made. Again there is useful discussion about the words they have used and the difference between books that will be read to their young audience and ones that some of them might soon be able to read for themselves.

There is great pride in the completed books which they take back to read to their partners. They enjoy the reaction particularly when they have incorporated the little ones' favourite games and their pets and they accept any criticisms that are made.

It can be more difficult to fit in activities such as this in today's more structured curriculum but there can still be a place for it. It can be undertaken under the Primary Liaison umbrella or as an activity focusing directly on improving literacy in your school. We have also offered it as a project during Activities Week. We work with the art department and offer it to Years 8 and 9. The procedure is the same but the final focus is not just on the words; we often have talented artists taking part who produce the most wonderful illustrations or use creative techniques like pop-ups and pull-outs.

17 Using novel openings

The introduction of the Literacy Strategy into secondary English classrooms has had a big impact on the way the subject is taught and much of the focus on word and sentence work has produced students who are more critical readers of their own and other people's writing. There have, however, been voices of concern about the way in which books have become vehicles for language study and a way of ticking off the National Curriculum reading requirements. Enjoyment of the book can be lost without a sense of the way in which the narrative drives the whole story and the ability to interact and empathize with the characters. David Almond, author of *Skellig*, is concerned about the way in which his book has become a source of examples of what verbs are and occasionally, how they work. Language work should be a way to enhance a reader's understanding and pleasure in a text; for inexperienced readers the concentration on detail can fragment any interest they had in the story.

Having said that, there are activities which can feed interest and still fulfil the requirement to read in detail. One of these is, I think, to look at openings and closures of novels. Debra Myhill writing in the *Secondary English* magazine in October 2001 uses this idea to teach the importance of the crafting of writing. This technique provides a manageable section of a variety of texts, provides tasters, and links the way that writers use detail to the strategies by which readers are hooked, as well as teaching student writers about how to craft their writing. I like the idea of using extracts of the text with a real purpose of the textual analysis being explicitly linked to the devices that encourage readers to read on.

The students are given a number of story openings; I usually use four and prefer to choose novels which I don't think that they will have read. They are then given some guidance on what to look for in their discussion. Is there a character or characters introduced? Is there any dialogue? Can you see any theme? Is there a clear setting? Is a problem presented? These focused them on some of the more frequent ways of opening stories. Here is the opening of *Pirates* by Celia Rees, one of the stories I have chosen.

Preface
1724

I write for many reasons.

I write, not least, to quiet my grief. I find that by reliving the adventures that I shared with Minerva, I can lessen the pain of our parting. Besides that, a long sea voyage can be tedious. I must find diversions that fit my station now that I have put up my pistols and cutlass and have exchanged my breeches for a dress.

What follows is my story. Mine and Minerva's. When I have finished writing down all that happened and how it came about, I plan to deliver my papers to Mr Daniel Defoe of London who, I understand, takes an interest in all those who have chosen to follow a piratical way of life.

The discussion of the questions above provided a focus when the class reported back and the following points were considered when the whole class became involved.

Pirates by Celia Rees

First-person, past-tense narrative. Introduces the central character and a companion, Minerva. Date and sea setting established with suggestion of character's involvement in piracy, probably at first hand. Emotional context with 'grief' and parting, but main character has come through difficult times and has come out the other side to adopt a different way of life. Not entirely happy about this, needs 'diversions' and comments on 'tedium' of sea voyage without 'cutlass and pistols'. Going to be an adventure story – unusual, with possibility of female pirate. Mention of Mr Defoe gives credibility but also links story with adventurous accounts like that of *Robinson Crusoe*.

The Garbage King by Elizabeth Laird was my second choice.

There was no light in the shack, none at all, except when the moon was shining. Mamo could see chinks of it then, through the gaps in the corrugated-iron roof.

But the moon wasn't out tonight. Mamo shivered, pulled the ragged blanket over his head and huddled against his sister's warm body. Tiggist had been facing away from him, but she turned over to lie on her back, the bare straw mattress rustling as she moved. He knew she was awake. He knew her eyes were open, and that she was staring up into the pitch-darkness.

'What are we going to do?' he said.

'I don't know.'

The Garbage King by Elizabeth Laird

Third-person, past-tense, omniscient narrator. Brother and sister Mamo and Tiggist introduced with the main focus on Mamo. Close relationship as he cuddles against her and knows she is awake without asking. Poverty of setting in 'shack', gaps in roof and 'ragged blanket' suggests a possible theme. Mamo's question introduces the idea that there is a difficulty to be resolved. Dialogue with his opening question suggests Tiggist is older and his belief that she will have answers to their problems. Her uncertainty shows that all won't be easily resolved.

Here is the opening to Catherine McPhail's *Underworld*.

'So, you haven't brought your PE kit again, Fiona?'

Fiona Duncan stood in front of the teacher, her very stance an act of defiance. Tapping her foot impatiently, balancing her bag on her hip. She made an art of looking bored, staring straight ahead, chewing her gum. She shrugged an answer.

Mr Marks looked just as bored. 'This is the third week in a row.'

'Really? I've not been counting myself.' Fiona's voice was full of sarcasm. That was what broke her teacher's temper at last.

'Yes, really! And this time you are in trouble.'

Fiona blew a bubble. 'Think so?'

'Yes, I think so, Fiona.'

Fiona didn't say anything for a moment, then her face creased into a triumphant smile. 'You can't make me do anything, sir.'

Underworld by Catherine McPhail

Third-person, past-tense narrative with an omniscient narrator. Establishes a good deal about both Fiona and Mr Marks and the relationship between them. Fiona is defiant and unbothered by the supposed authority of her teacher. She is bright and uses sarcasm to defend herself. Physical description of her behaviour, the tapping foot, reinforces her words. School setting and situation of PE lesson is familiar. Use of short interchanges in dialogue gives realism. Fiona's triumph and idea that teacher is powerless suggests that a possible plot might develop to show opposite.

The final opening is from *Montmorency* by Eleanor Updale.

1815: The Bloody Beginning

The pain woke him again. Not the constant throb that was so familiar he could hardly remember being without it. This was one of those sharp stabs from the wound along his thigh. Doctor Farcett had dug deep to get through to the shattered bone, and the layers of catgut stitching pulled as the torn flesh struggled to realign itself inside. After so many interventions by the keen young medic, Montmorency should have been prepared for the agony, but each time the after-effects seemed worse, and the limited pain relief (alcohol, and the occasional treat of an experimental gas) less effective.

The candle on the central table had burned almost to nothing: it must be nearly morning, but there was no sign of light through the bars high up in the wall. Montmorency knew there was no point in calling for the night guard. Marston, silent, still, and unsmiling, saw his duties in the prison hospital as strictly limited to preventing escapes. Never mind the fact that Montmorency couldn't even turn over in bed, let alone run away. He'd have to wait in the dark for the arrival of Nurse Darnley, a brusque but well-meaning woman who believed that bad people could be made good and that providing a sip of water to a sick criminal might help that process.

Montmorency by Eleanor Updale

Third-person, past-tense, omniscient narrator. Date and hospital setting established first, prison through detail of the bars and the guard. Short opening sentence establishes the importance of the pain and its significance. Questions aroused about the need for regular surgery, the cause of injury and why Montmorency is in prison. Characters drawn lightly, Marston's keenness, nurse's kindness. Sympathy created for Montmorency with constant pain, description of operation without anaesthesia and 'throb', 'sharp pain' and 'agony'.

This activity can be developed in a number of ways. I often now ask students which story they would like to continue reading and why. I find it a useful task to do early in the year to help establish reading patterns. It can then lead into a writing task: sometimes they continue the story by crafting the next page or two. They have to use what they have learned about the characters and their situations to move the stories on. This frees many writers who can develop the ideas without having to know how to resolve them. They can choose to focus on what they have learned about the characters or the situation, or they can develop any of the plot ideas that appeal. They also have to look carefully at any stylistic features they have noted and try to emulate them, for example, the very sarcastic tone of exchange between Fiona and Mr Marks. The difficulty often lies in persuading them not to finish the stories in the next two pages!

An alternative writing task is to get them to write their own opening of a story using what they have learned about what is to be found there.

Debra Myhill then continues with looking at the closures. Students are given the ends of the novels and asked to try to match the end with the beginning using any of the clues of cohesion. Names do give the game away but students who only use names can be persuaded to move beyond that to find other cohesive devices.

In looking at closures students are given another set of questions:

- Does the story still seem to be in the same genre or about the same topic?
- Can you see the closure of a problem? Are any loose ends tied up? Are you left wondering about what might happen next?
- Are there any words or phrases in the final section which echo those in the opening?
- Is there any sort of message given in the final words?

So in case you want to follow the pattern, let's look at the closures. Here is the end of *Pirates*:

We are nearing the Western Approaches now, and it will not be long before we sight England. I own to feelings of great excitement and anticipation, and even greater nervousness. But I am resolved. When we dock in London, I will deliver these papers to Mr Defoe. Then I intend to find William, and to marry him, if he will still have me. And after that? You may wish me luck, or curse me for a damnable pirate, but do not look for me. I will be gone to parts beyond the sea.

Pirates

Link back to the Preface at the end of the long sea voyage. Repeat of the determination to give the story she has written to Mr Defoe. Tedium of sea voyage is over and grief at parting from Minerva is replaced by 'excitement and anticipation' at finding William, hopefully for marriage, so the end is positive and up-beat. Final two sentences are well balanced, one long with three parts, and with reader involvement in wishing luck or cursing (Echoes of Prospero's request for the 'gentle breath' of his audience to fill his sails) and a short one with a sense of being out of reach and gone to a better life.

The end of *The Garbage King* is rather different:

'I suppose I'd better go home,' he said.
'Me too,' said Dani.
They shook hands with a kind of formality. Dani punched Mamo lightly on the shoulder, and Mamo buffeted Dani back.
'I'll see you around,' said Dani.
'Yes,' said Mamo, and he turned and walked quickly away, whistling between his teeth as he went.

The Garbage King

This seems a different Mamo from the beginning. The frightened boy relying on his sister for what to do has been replaced by a more confident, independent one 'whistling between his teeth'. Tiggest is no longer here. The relationship between Dani and Mamo seems strong, shown by this double leavetaking. The contrast of the more adult formality of shaking hands with the boyish 'buffeting' implies a wish to remain together or at least to maintain the relationship. Both opening and closing use physical details to give reality to the characters. Seems a positive ending but when Mamo turns away from Dani's suggestion that he will see him around could suggest uncertainty.

Here is the ending of *Underworld*:

I am an old man now. If I write my story, who would believe me? And do I believe it now myself? It is only an old legend. A story told around the camp fires on a dark night.
  So long ago.

Yet, I will never forget the terrified eyes of my Captain as the mouth of the Worm closed on him.

Underworld

This could be the ending of a completely different novel. The opening suggested a school story with problems between students and teachers. This sounds more like a fantasy adventure story. Third-person narrative is now first-person with no indication of who the narrator is. This section comes in a different font set apart completely from the rest of the text and suggests a much later period and with the mention of legend is perhaps a story that will be told repeatedly rather than one rooted in the here and now as the opening suggested.

Finally, here is the end section of *Montmorency*:

The authorities were relieved too. Sir Gordon's death meant there was no need for a trial, and the full details of the Mauramanian plot could remain a secret. Luckily for the Foreign Secretary, his loan from the traitor stayed a secret too. He never had to pay it back, and basked in the goodwill of the Prime Minister and the Queen, who were jubilant at the way he had solved such a potentially explosive situation so quietly.

And so Montmorency put another world behind him. Though under the bed in his room at Bargles lay a splendid pair of waders. He told one of the Sams that he was preparing for a fishing trip to Scotland. He told himself that they were souvenirs.

But in his heart he knew why he was keeping them.

Just in case.

Montmorency, still the central character, clearly has been freed from prison and been involved in some political escapade which has resulted in his rehabilitation. The words 'plot' and 'traitor' with their hints of intrigue and the reference to the Foreign Secretary solving an 'explosive situation' suggest a spy or thriller story with Montmorency as some sort of undercover agent. The reference to 'just in case' suggests that further adventures will be developed.

If the activity is developed as a writing task the students can now be given time to finish writing their own stories. They now have their own collection of techniques to use and can explain when they have finished how they had crafted the openings and closings and any links that they have created between them. They have used the texts carefully to analyse the writer's techniques but not in isolation and many of them go on to read the remainder of the books after this exercise.

Part Four

Wider Opportunities

18 Reading challenges

The competitive element of reading challenges, devised to encourage reading for pleasure, often has great appeal for boys in particular. Many schools use schemes of their own to set out their expectations early on in secondary school. These are often booklets with suggested reading activities, some to be completed for homework, some in English lessons or the library and some to encourage and support the students' own private reading. These are often designed with the National Curriculum statement on encouraging 'independent reading' in mind.

The schemes need to be flexible, to stretch the most able but to allow success for the least able. Care is needed as many students who find reading difficult and 'boring' are already aware of their inadequacies and need not to be identified by their lack of success. The scheme needs to show progression for the reader, to show a reader's response to what they have read, to broaden the scope for readers by introducing them to genres and authors that they might not otherwise choose and to make targets for them.

Let me outline the scheme that we use: we have used this for some years now, updating the reading lists on a regular basis. This is the pattern that we follow (see overleaf).

All students take part in this scheme and homework time is given over to it. They all begin by reading a book of their choice to get a Bronze sticker. This can be a speed read, a picture book, a graphic novel, or for finishing the book that they are currently reading. We try to focus on fiction but teachers use their discretion depending on the interests of the students. This free choice is to try to involve everyone.

The second level is Silver and this means choosing two books from our Silver list of which all students have a copy. This means that we can include titles which may be in the town library or

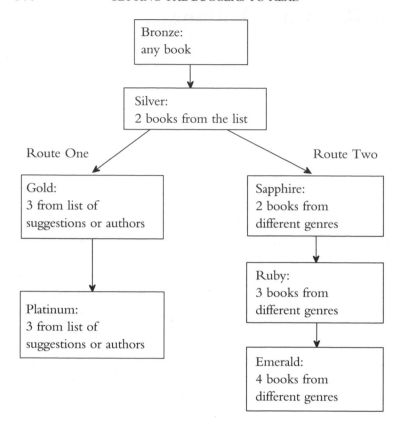

Figure 3 Reading challenges

which students may have at home. Incidentally, this often encourages students to network in sharing books. Some are also available in class libraries. We try to make the list as comprehensive as possible, adding new titles as EXTRAS on display in the library. The books are identified by silver stars on the spines so they are easily recognized. This is where it is important for teachers to be flexible. The books on the Silver list are wide-ranging teenage novels but, to involve all students, do include authors like Roald Dahl and Dick King-Smith and some *Goosebumps* and *Captain Underpants* for weaker readers. For students who 'don't read books' we encourage the use of audio tapes, providing the facilities to listen in the resource centre to get them started. It is also an opportunity to use paired reading in an informal way either with older students (our sixth-form support classes for community service are invaluable here) or with pairs of students in the class.

After the Silver level the routes diverge; Route One involves two more levels, Gold and Platinum and here the texts become increasingly challenging. Often there are only authors or suggestions for texts; only our very committed readers tend to take this route. The alternative, Route Two, divides books into genres and tries to broaden the scope of students' reading. Their booklet gives illustrations of the possible genres they can read and suggestions of titles. Here are the genre lists for fantasy and war stories:

War Stories

Ted Allebury	*As Time Goes By*
Andrew Davies	*Conrad's War*
Terry Deary	*True War Stories*
Ellis Dillon	*Children of Bach*
Michael Foreman	*War Boy*
Anne Frank	*The Diary of Anne Frank*
Bette Green	*Summer of My German Soldier*
Elizabeth Laird	*On the Run*
Michelle Magorian	*Goodnight, Mister Tom*
Michael Morpugo	*War Horse*
	Private Peaceful
Gary Paulsen	*The Rifle*
Bill Rosen	*Swallows in Winter*
Robert Westall	*Echoes of War*
	Gulf

Fantasy Stories

David Almond	*Skellig*
Lynne Reid Banks	*Melusine*
Helen Cresswell	*Ellie and the Hagwitch*

Helen Cresswell	*Moondial*
Cornelia Funke	*Inkheart*
Neil Gaimon	*Coraline*
Alan Garner	*Elidor*
C. S. Lewis	*The Lion, the Witch and the Wardrobe*
Jenny Nimmo	*Griffin's Castle*
Garth Nix	*Sabriel*
Mary Norton	*The Borrowers*
Philippa Pearce	*Tom's Midnight Garden*
Marcus Sedgewick	*The Dark Horse*
J. R. R. Tolkein	*The Hobbit*

It is always possible to come up with other options and students often come up with alternatives which are much better for them. Using the genre route means that students can tailor their reading to their own level and follow particular interests and, although the texts may not be as challenging, they read more of them.

This is all very well but how do we know that the students have actually read the books they say they have? It is necessary to devise a process of checking, preferably one which is fun and easy to do and which doesn't involve the teacher in a great deal of extra marking as avid readers devour books very quickly, particularly when there is an incentive.

Suggestions for Reporting Back on Books

- The students themselves could make their own list of criteria of what makes a good book, which they agree and all use to make their judgements.
- Put students in small groups which have to record a presentation on the books that they have read. They should explain why they liked the book and read a sample of a particularly good part. The others in the group can then ask questions. Make short tapes of particularly effective story openings as tasters for others (*Witch Child* by Celia Rees is a good example here).

- Write a letter to a character in the book commenting on what he/she has experienced.
- Writing book reviews which are then displayed in the library and/or classroom (the NATE magazine is a good source of models for these).
- Write a letter to the author giving your opinion of the book. Send these if at all possible. Publishers will forward letters; authors like to receive them and the majority reply.
- Any of the activities in the private reading section might be appropriate here.

Another way of setting a reading challenge is to buy into a scheme such as the Accelerated Reader scheme from Renaissance Publishing. This offers a diagnostic service as well as a method of encouraging wider reading. It involves students in making choices with a personal sense of challenge too. It uses a computer programme to test their understanding and allows teachers to use the results as well as giving each student an individual printout to show how well they've done. The initial package which we bought with education learning credits comes with 100 quizzes which you can choose from a list of more than 1,000 titles. We bought a further 300 quizzes this year so that we could extend our target audience.

We began by introducing the scheme to a Year 8 group using a smart board to demonstrate a quiz to the whole group. We chose a Harry Potter title that many of them had read or had recently seen the film. This was useful as it showed them that seeing a film did not really give the level of detail necessary to answer the questions. We then gave each student a copy of the list of titles, showing the level of difficulty and the points to be gained from each one. It took some time to help them select a book which was appropriate for them. Some wanted to read books which were far below their ability and liked the sense of immediate success but soon realized that they gained very few points that way. It is possible to run the scheme in a number of ways: individual students can be set targets, students may be grouped with a target for the group, or you can set a class target over a particular period.

When each student has read a book they take a quiz on the computer to see how well they have understood what they have read. The questions are quite challenging and for higher points students may need to read at quite a sophisticated level. The points they are given are pro rata for the number of questions correctly answered. If insufficient questions are attempted or too many mistakes are made the students receive no points to add to their score. Each student is given an individual printout addressed to them with praise for their efforts or commiseration if their score is below the 60 per cent necessary to pass. Students then keep these in a folder and can chart their progress on a record sheet.

Reporting back on this is also useful for the teacher. A report sheet can be printed which shows how many quizzes each individual student has taken and the percentage of correct scores for each one. This makes it possible to give advice about which books might be less or more of a challenge as necessary.

It is clear that there are disadvantages to this system. All the students like working on the computers and some will try to answer quizzes on books that either they read last year or which they haven't yet finished. This does distort the group score and make it difficult for you to use the results diagnostically to suggest what they might read next. We found it difficult to run with the initial 100 quizzes and, if you can afford it, I would advise starting with the 300 pack too. You also need to choose your titles very carefully to ensure that you cover all tastes and all abilities. We found that we had too many grouped in the middle. To ensure that some of our weaker readers could take part we used audio books which still allows them to answer the questions. If you run a paired reading scheme the selected titles could be available there too.

Once the system is up and running and the students understand what to do, it is possible for the students to take the quizzes at any point. Students can use lunchtimes if they have access to computers or, if you have availability in your classroom, they can use a few minutes at the ends of lessons to complete them. The printout provides a record for them and they can use this to complete their own reading record of everything that they read with a total of their points' score. The competitive element of this often appeals to the more reluctant boys. The glory of it is that once you have set it up it is also a useful homework task which carries with it its own built-in checking system in the form of the quizzes.

Many secondary schools provide challenges which build on those offered by local libraries. In Cambridgeshire a Reading Rollercoaster challenges youngsters to read six books over the summer holidays providing stickers and certificates for the 5,000 who take up the challenge.

19 Reading groups

The burgeoning popularity of reading groups over recent years is something we can take advantage of in school. Groups can be set up to indulge specific tastes such as science fiction, crime fiction and teenage fiction or to broaden the scope of students' reading. They can be cross-age groups, as in shadowing the Carnegie Award, or in a particular age group. These don't have to be run only by members of English departments. Many staff have reading passions which they would be only too happy to share. Sometimes you might have to set up a staff one to accommodate all the volunteers!

Setting up a reading group is straightforward. You first need to decide on your subject and target audience. We decided to set one up with the sixth year and try to tap into students who don't necessarily take English at A-level. Initial advertising was in assembly and fliers through tutor groups but the group has grown since then. In our first brief meeting in school the students decided on the timing and date of the first meeting and the first book. The selection of material has been great and can introduce you to authors you don't know. The students do make it very much their own and the group has developed a strong identity. These are the books we read during the first year:

Captain Corelli's Mandolin	Louis de Bernieres
Mort	Terry Pratchett
The Woman in Black	Susan Hill
The Crow Road	Iain Banks
The Deadly Space Between	Patricia Duncker
Border Crossing	Pat Barker
Emma	Jane Austen
Trainspotting	Irvine Welch
The Wasp Factory	Iain Banks

The final two were summer reading so that we could start immediately we went back in the new term. The students suggested that the week of our upcoming Ofsted inspection would be good timing which proved to be true as we were joined by our designated inspector who enjoyed the lively discussion of *Trainspotting*. Student choices like this can be very salutary for the teacher. I had to confess to not finishing the book, something which happens to me fairly rarely, and I had to defend my decision against a spirited attack from most of the students who had enjoyed it.

There was a small core of five students who attended regularly and three or four more who came occasionally. That was during the first year and we were then joined by six lower-sixth who made up a larger group. Ten or 12 makes for an even livelier discussion. Even the decision on which books to read next becomes more interesting as the students range over classics and modern novels which they have heard discussed.

The second year saw a broader selection, including some which were being discussed everywhere:

Catch 22	Joseph Heller
1984	George Orwell
and	
Brave New World	Aldous Huxley
The Curious Incident of the Dog in the Night-time	Mark Haddon
Vernon God Little	D. B. C. Pierre
The Handmaid's Tale	Margaret Atwood
The Life of Pi	Yann Martel
Notes from a Scandal	Zoe Heller
Noughts and Crosses	Malorie Blackman
Five People That You Meet in Heaven	Mick Albon
A Fine Balance	Rohinton Mistry
The Reader	Bernard Schlink
Tales of the City	Armistead Maupin

The meetings take place after school once a month and last for about an hour, although sometimes it is much longer; the Patricia

Duncker and Zoe Heller kept us in school until nearly 6 pm! The discussion on the latter was fascinating as the perspectives of two female teachers were radically different from the teenagers. To ensure informality we have tea and biscuits and the students are planning a theatre trip to London to see *The Woman In Black* next term.

The group grew by word of mouth when students realized that they weren't being asked to read 'great literature' but could choose what they wanted to read. Some lively discussion has come from choosing which books to read but in general they are very open. Some groups take it in turns to choose but ours like the discussions of what might be a good choice for the group to read next. Not all of the group are students who will continue with English studies but all are very committed readers. One was working her way through the books on The Big Read list!

It is the community of readers who can share their enthusiasms that is so valuable here. The students discuss the books with confidence within the meetings but also outside so other people see these enthusiasms validated and are sometimes sparked to read the books they are discussing. Some of the students who have joined us have come primarily because of these conversations. On a very practical note too, these students can include this on UCAS application forms.

It is possible that there are funds in school to support groups like this. All schools have received money that can be spent on study support – activities like reading clubs that take place out of normal school hours. Generally, students buy their own books as most like to keep them, but occasionally during the year we offer some subsidies; the ability to buy the books should not be a criterion for joining the group, and some of the group will happily borrow from others.

An obvious spin-off from this would be to set up a lower school group using keen older students, maybe Years 12 or 10 to work with 7, 8 and 9. Sixth-form boys with Year 8 and 9 boys might be particularly effective in helping to maintain enthusiasm for books among those groups where it can wane. The groups can be advertised with specific themes in mind and even if a theme, such as fantasy, is chosen it could help to broaden the scope of their reading beyond Harry Potter and *The Lord of the Rings*.

Shadowing the Carnegie Award provides another sort of reading group and once students have got the taste for this many of them would like to continue.

20 Libraries

What I have tried to do so far in this book is make suggestions and references to the activities in which teachers and schools engage to persuade our students that they want to read. There are mentions of the role of the school library, or resource centre as many have now become, but I now want to deal with that in some more detail.

The role of the resource centre in supporting reading extends far beyond the work of the English department, although working together means that more can take place when you use the skills of the librarians. It mirrors the role of public libraries in our society with many of the same aims. Because anyone can borrow books without charge or judgement it provides an opportunity for young people to experiment with their reading without pressure or risk. This is always clear to me when we shadow the Carnegie Award. When I write to parents to sanction Year 7 reading young adult titles, the students always accept this but most say that their parents allow them to choose books for themselves without checking them first. When they borrow from the library there is no pressure on them to conform to expectations.

Although most English departments, if not individual class-rooms, have access to a selection of reading material, libraries are much better equipped with a range of reading material. They can also access material from a national network to supplement themed reading or to provide multiple copies of books. Again, the Carnegie Shadowing scheme is a good example here for it couldn't take place for the number of interested readers unless the local library service provided extra copies of the short-listed books.

The staff in a good library are also highly skilled in active encouragement of young people's reading. There will always be someone, in a public library, who specializes in young people's literature and can recommend alternative texts if they are told which genre is preferred. They have access to a wide range of support material from national services which can help to broaden horizons without any commercial or educational pressures and they are aware of the curriculum demands on young people and can help them to plan accordingly.

The library can also help you to plan projects. You may be able to borrow a selection of different texts to try out with a class. Some libraries are able to offer loans of small sets of texts, perfect if you are just starting out on Guided Reading and you want to give the students in your group different texts. This would allow you to try them out before you commit money to them. Also, you can often borrow themed sets of books to support work on a particular subject. For example, working on *Romeo and Juliet* with Year 10 you might decide to create an essay for coursework on the theme of conflict in literature. The ability of the group will determine how you deal with this but you could include non-fiction material on real events in history, for example, Martin Luther King's speech. A themed box might include a breadth of material to appeal to a mixed-ability audience and give students greater commitment to the task if they have chosen their own texts from a selection.

Conflict

The Fire Eaters	David Almond
When the Wind Blows	Raymond Briggs
The Chocolate War	Robert Cormier
To Kill a Mocking Bird	Harper Lee
The Other Side of Truth	Beverley Naidoo
The Wind Singer	William Nicholson
Wolf Brother	Michelle Paver
The Catcher in the Rye	J. D. Salinger
Maus (I and II)	Art Spiegelmann
Roll of Thunder Hear my Cry	Mildred Taylor
Gulf	Robert Westall

The school library is also invaluable in setting up any of the reading challenges you might wish to use. We bought the Accelerated Reading in conjunction with the library and it was the librarian who presented it to the students through an interactive whiteboard. This uses the expertise of one person so that staff involved in the scheme could use it immediately with classes rather than each individual needing to master the process before they could begin. The selection of texts for the scheme was done jointly so that we could cross-match what was in the library with our preferred choices. Finally, the librarian distributed the assessment sheets for the students and collated the information on class reading for each member of staff, thus allowing them to use it to help readers to move on.

Many public libraries provide other services too. They may be involved in booking authors and you can tap into this. For example, Remembrance Day is being celebrated in North-amptonshire this year with a visit from Theresa Breslin talking about her book *Remembrance* which deals with the fortunes of four young people caught up in the Great War. It is worth developing a relationship with your local library for information about visits like this.

Their website www.northamptonshire.gov.uk/Reading+Really +Matters/Homepage.htm is also worth a look as it is another source of links to author websites. The one on Neil Gaiman's *Coraline* and *The Tales of the Otori* are both really good at providing tasters and enticements to read.

Another scheme adopted in many areas is the summer reading scheme which challenges students to read a number of different books and rewards them with a a certificate of excellence on completion, and it is interesting to see how many Year 7 and perhaps Year 8 students have been involved with this. Bringing together different sections of their lives like this is a way of helping young people to make sense of the whole and to recognize that there are some common goals shared by school and society outside.

21 Creating buyers of books

Students talking about influences on their reading often cite parents as particularly important as they are often a good source of providing books. Many of my really avid readers say that their parents will nearly always agree when asked to buy them a book while other items are often refused. Parents want their children to be readers knowing that the ability to read well has a profound effect on their education. This encourages children to see themselves as owners of books and many express a preference for owning their own books rather than using the library or borrowing them. This allows them to choose exactly when to begin reading, to take how long they want over the book and to re-read if they want to. There is also the added pleasure of the smell of new books and the crispness of pages unopened by anyone else.

For these reasons I try to provide opportunities in school to allow students to become buyers and to see themselves as people who choose to buy books for pleasure. This is particularly useful for students from families who don't necessarily have this tradition. One way of doing this is to use a book club like Scholastic. They have been running for a long time now and have tailored their offers to very specific age groups. We use the Cover to Cover leaflets which are aimed at secondary students. The leaflets are bright and colourful and are useful in a number of ways. They make a good lesson to encourage networking. I issue the leaflets and allow a few minutes to browse while I listen to the reactions. This allows me to gauge what is currently popular. We then roam through the leaflets and discuss anything on there which any of the students have already read. Some have read other books by the same author (any new Jacqueline Wilson is always enthusiastically received) and recommendations and cautions are given.

Support is given when setting up with Scholastic with advice on how to administer the scheme and a description of how it benefits the school. Discount is given in the form of vouchers which can be used to buy from the leaflets or from the teachers' list. The most significant point is that there is no obligation for students to buy more than once if they don't want to; in that way it is not like a traditional book club. It has the added benefit for you in that the orders can now be sent on the Internet which makes it much quicker and easier.

I hope that this doesn't sound too commercial to you and I know that the union restrictions on taking money may put some of you off. I have found that the regular chance for students to recommend books to each other helps to develop a reading community and the excitement when they arrive offsets the work involved in organizing it.

Another way of encouraging students to be book buyers is to run a bookshop in school. This can be a fixture if you have space to put it but the easier way is to invite in a local bookshop. World Book day, a day during a reading festival or the run up to Christmas can all be suitable occasions. It is important to discuss with the bookshop staff specific age groups that you are interested in and if possible give them a copy of any booklist that you issue in school, in advance of the visit. Students could also be invited to suggest books that they would like to see in the shop. You need to publicize the shop well in advance in school, and inform parents of the date and times of opening. Some of the parents would like to come in so it is useful to try to site the shop somewhere easily accessible. If it is near Christmas or just before the end of the summer term it's possible to provide an adult selection for present buying and holiday reading too. There can be a spin-off too from this in a discount which you can use to buy books to top up reading boxes.

We have also found it useful to have a bookshop on certain open evenings. A Year 7 parents'/carers' evening early in the autumn term is an opportunity to alert parents to our reading scheme. We have the booklist available and a bookshop with staff who can discuss the books on the list and make recommendations. We display lists of the major book prize winners and try to have copies for sale and show reviews of books by Year 7 students.

As Year 7 students also show parents around there are often students available to enthuse about their latest favourites. We repeat this on an evening for Year 10 parents, which is designed to help them support their children through the GCSE course. Parents are given a brief talk on how to encourage reading and again we provide a list of suggested titles. The shop provides fiction, reference books and study aids to support their work in school.

The wealth of support on the Internet for reading can make it difficult to know where to go so I have tried to find websites which can be genuinely helpful. My Home Library at www.myhomelibrary.org, endorsed by Anne Fine, is a website dedicated to encouraging young people to enjoy owning their own books. It has a wonderful selection of bookplates to download by a variety of illustrators in both colour and black and white which can be coloured in. The plates are different sizes and the idea is to make children proud of owning their own book collection by naming them. Anne Fine champions the use of second-hand bookshops and charity shops like Oxfam as a source for improving students' own collections. The bookplates can then be used to cover up the names of the previous owners. The site also gives tips on finding books for budding collectors, like asking for favourite authors or missing titles in a series, as charity shops often cannot keep all their stock on display. While many adults would like young people to read the classics, *Robinson Crusoe* or *Treasure Island*, Anne Fine recommends more modern classics, like *The Wolves of Willoughby Chase* by Joan Aiken, *Jennings* by Antony Buckeridge or Roger Lancelyn Green's version of the *Tales of Robin Hood*, which youngsters can still find in second-hand shops.

All of these suggestions encourage them to become owners and to take pride in their ownership of books.

Collection of Modern Classics

Over Sea, Under Stone	Susan Cooper (there are 4 more in the series)
Elidor	Alan Garner
The Owl Service	Alan Garner

Tom's Midnight Garden	Philippa Pearce (try anything by her)
The Borrowers	Mary Norton
The Secret Garden	Frances Hodgson Burnett
The Chocolate War	Robert Cormier
The Once and Future Kin	T. H. White
I Capture the Castle	Dodie Smith
Moondial	Helen Cresswell

22 Key Stage 5

Most of the suggestions for texts that I have made have been suitable for approximately 11–16 year olds with some distinction made for titles which are more suitable for older ones. One area that I have not dealt with is those texts which move young people from teenage to adult literature. Some current novels are now being marketed in this area as cross-over texts: Mark Haddon's Whit-bread winner, *The Curious Incident of the Dog in the Night-time* and Jennifer Donnelly's Carnegie winner, *A Gathering Light* to name but two. This can be quite a difficult area to negotiate as once students have the reading ability and stamina to choose from any area they are often left to fend for themselves. Parents often ask for booklists as they have personal preferences but are not sure what is available. Year 12 students taking A-level also often need advice about what they might enjoy if they have any time left after work!

One way we found round this was to produce a booklet entitled *The English Department Recommends*. Each of us undertook to choose five books which we would suggest to sixth-form students. We wrote a brief description and explained our reasons for choosing them. The choices ranged across genres and included classics and page turners, for example *Heart of Darkness, Emma, Madame Bovary* to *The Mists of Avalon* (Marion Bradley's version of Arthurian legend written from the point of view of the women who were involved). These were printed with glossy covers and each of our A-level students received one. They were the source of some interesting conversations with students not only about our choices but also some astute comments about what these choices said about the staff. Many of them did try some of the books that were recommended there and later comments about the books were also tempered with 'I can see why she would have chosen that'. It also allowed us to open up wider issues for discussion with our students. Novelists do go in and out of fashion and some of our choices may well belong to this category. We discussed which ones they thought might remain on lists of favourites and why. One reason cited for possible disappearance was that books which had enjoyed commercial success were often incompatible with literary success.

There is a bit of a grey area for boys who continue to read beyond 14. The young adult titles seem to be more aimed at girls with the exception perhaps of Melvyn Burgess and Robert Cormier. We are often so relieved that they are still reading that what they read seems irrelevant; however many boys, who are not sci-fi or fantasy readers, go straight to adult thrillers or crime novels with their violent depictions of women as victims. I am always trying to add to my list books that they can enjoy but which have perhaps a wider and less bleak view of the world. Love stories written from a male perspective have always been in short supply but Nick Hornby and Tony Parsons are helping here. The readers group, like the one we run for Years 12 and 13 students, also helps to broaden the scope of their reading and not only for students who might want to read English at university. This encourages reading of the texts that are currently under discussion in the press or talked about by friends or parents. The main message here is to keep talking about books, particularly the ones that a wide range of people find interesting. They may be books that you have enjoyed or, if you have disliked something that is currently very popular, it can be a spur to provoke discussion.

For students studying A-level English, another possible way of broadening scope is to use a coursework option, if it is available, in both Years 12 and 13, to encourage students to choose their own texts to study. They need support in choosing appropriate texts to satisfy A-level criteria, but they do work with real interest on creating writing titles for these texts. They can read individual texts, work on a theme across a number of texts on the work of a particular author. This allows them to validate their choices and bring their own enthusiasm to the subject. Any text which is judged to have sufficient value for study at this level is acceptable and the texts read can considerably broaden A-level study.

23 Final thoughts

I have tried to do two things in this book: recognize the need to improve the literacy level of all of the students that we teach and also to convey the pleasure and enjoyment in reading a good book. The level of literacy as measured at Key Stage 3 tests is seen to be a clearer indicator of GCSE grades in most subjects than any other marker. Although literacy can clearly not be the responsibility of the English department alone we can help students' literacy development by creating enthusiasm for the pleasure that books and words can bring. I hope that focusing on ways of encouraging readers and promoting reading, and legitimizing and supporting the choices that they make, will help to give students the confidence necessary to become lifelong readers as well as bringing about improvements.

I hope that you find something here that will help you to promote reading for your students; the greatest effect that you can have is to communicate your own enthusiasm for books and to fire your students with it.

Appendix

Book suggestions

If you liked

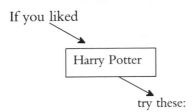

Harry Potter

try these:

The Book of Three	Lloyd Alexander
Artemis Fowl	Eoin Colfer
The Ghost Drum	Susan Cooper
The Witches	Roald Dahl
Dragon Rider	Cornelia Funke
The Weirstone of Brisingamen	Alan Garner
Stravaganza: City of Masks	Mary Hoffman
Arthur: The Seeing Stone	Kevin Crossley-Holland
Not Just a Witch	Eva Ibbotson
Redwall	Brian Jacques
The Phantom Tollbooth	Norton Juster
A Wrinkle in Time	Madeline L'Engle
The Akhenaten Adventure	P. B. Kerr
The Lion, the Witch and the Wardrobe	C. S. Lewis
The Giver	Lois Lowry
The Enchanted Castle	E. E. Nesbit
Midnight for Charlie Bone	Jenny Nimmo
The Wee Free Men	Terry Pratchett
The Book of Dead Days	Marcus Sedgewick
The Amulet of Samarkand	Jonathon Stroud
The Changeover	Margaret Mahy
Wicca series	Cate Tierney

Older readers

Over Sea, Under Stone	Susan Cooper
Across the Nightingale Floor	Lian Hearn
The Wizard of Earthsea	Ursula Le Guin
Gathering Blue	Lois Lowry
The Changeover	Margaret Mahy
The Wind Singer	William Nicolson
Sabriel	Garth Nix
The Hounds of the Morrigan	Pat O'Shea
Circle of Magic	Tamora Pierce
His Dark Materials	Philip Pullman
Witch Child	Celia Rees
The Dark Horse	Martin Sedgewick
The Lord of the Rings	J. R. R. Tolkien

If you liked

> *Goodnight Mr Tom*
> Michelle Magorian

try these:

Key Stage 3

War Horse	Michael Morpurgo	WWI
Private Peaceful	Michael Morpurgo	
Friedrich	Hans Peter Richter	WWII
Carrie's War	Nina Bawden	
I am David	Anne Holm	
War Boy	Michael Foreman	
Kensuke's Kingdom	Michael Morpurgo	
The Diary of Anne Frank	Anne Frank	
The Silver Sword	Ian Serraillier	
Milkweed	Jerry Spinelli	

Other historical novels

The True Confessions of Charlotte Doyle	Avi	
The Fire-Eaters	David Almond	Cuban missile crisis
King of Shadows	Susan Cooper	Shakespeare's time

The Midwife's Apprentice	Karen Cushman	Medieval life
Coram Boy	Jamila Gavin	18th century
Ruby in the Smoke	Philip Pullman	19th century
Pirates	Celia Rees	
Cue for Treason	Geoffrey Trease	
Grace	Jill Paton Walsh	

Key Stage 4

When the Wind Blows	Raymond Biggs	WWII
Remembrance	Theresa Breslin	WWI
Heroes	Robert Cormier	WWII
The Kin	Peter Dickinson	
Smith	Leon Garfield	
Troy	Adele Geras	
Across the Barricades	Joan Lingard	Northern Ireland
The Shell House	Linda Newbury	
Some Other War	Linda Newbury	
Nightjohn	Gary Paulson	
Final Journey	Gudrun Pausewang	Holocaust
The Sterkarm Handshake	Susan Price	Time travel
Milkweed	Jerry Spinelli	

If you like to travel

try these:

Books with a strong evocation of place

Key Stage 3

The Garbage King	Elizabeth Laird	Ethiopia
A Journey to the River Sea	Eva Ibbotson	South America
The Thief Lord	Cornelia Funke	Venice
Kensuke's Kingdom	Michael Morpurgo	Desert island in the Pacific ocean
Plundering Paradise	Geraldine McCaughrean	Madagascar
Gulf	Robert Westall	Set in the Gulf War
Red Dog	Louis de Bernieres	Australia

Key Stage 4

No 1 Ladies' Detective Agency	James Alexander McCall Smith	Africa
Roll of Thunder Hear My Cry	Mildred Taylor	Southern states of America – good too for history of racism in America
Talking in Whispers	James Watson	Chile in Pinochet's time
Hideous Kinky	Esther Feud	Morocco
Skindeep	Toecky Jones	South Africa
The Frozen Waterfall	Gaye Hicyilmaz	This begins in Turkey, then moves to Switzerland. It makes interesting contrasts between them
Bury the Dead	Peter Carter	Berlin before the wall came down

Key Stage 3

The Witch of Blackbird Pond	Elizabeth Speare	American exploration
The Ballad of Lucy Whipple	Karen Cushman	American exploration

If you are interested in science

try these:

Key Stage 3

The Monster Garden	Vivien Alcock
When the Wind Blows	Raymond Briggs
Silent Spring	Rachel Carson (this is old but still great)
Empty World	John Christopher

Eva	Peter Dickinson
Dr Franklin's Island	Ann Halam
The Weather Eye	Lesley Howarth
The Giver	Lois Lowry
Speaking to Miranda	Caroline MacDonald
Shade's Children	Garth Nix
Z for Zachariah	Robert O'Brien
Mrs Frisby and the Rats of Nimh	Robert O'Brien
Mortal Engines	Philip Reeve
The Speed of the Dark	Alan Shearer
Plague 99	Jean Ure

Key Stage 4

The Plague Dogs	Richard Adams
The Foundation trilogy	Isaac Asimov
The Death of Grass	John Christopher
A Bone from the Sea	Peter Dickinson
Frankenstein	Mary Shelley
On the Beach	Nevil Shute
Brother in the Land	Robert Swindells
Journey to the Centre of the Earth	Jules Verne
The Plague Dogs	Richard Adams

If you liked

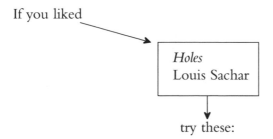

> *Holes*
> Louis Sachar

try these:

Flight #116 Is Down	Caroline B. Cooney
Tenderness: A Novel	Robert Cormier
Julie of the Wolves	Jean Craighead George
Ruby Holler	Sharon Creech
The Edge	Alan Gibbons
Wreckers	Iain Lawrence
Children of the Dust	Louise Lawrence
Letters from the Inside	John Marsden

Kensuke's Kingdom	Michael Morpurgo
Harris and Me	Gary Paulson
Hatchet	Gary Paulson
Are you in the house alone?	Richard Peck
Broken Bridge	Lynne Reid Banks
Free Fall	Joyce Sweeney
When She Hollers	Cynthia Voigt
The Machine Gunners	Robert Westall
The Cay	Theodore Taylor

If you like crime stories

try these:

Key Stage 3

The Thief Lord	Cornelia Funke
Monster	Walter Dean Myers
Baa, Baa Dead Sheep	Jill Bennett
Montmorency	Eleanor Updale
The Ruby in the Smoke	Philip Pullman
The Dance of the Assassins	Hervé Jubert
Scorpia	Anthony Horowirz

Key Stage 4

Tenderness	Robert Cormier
We All Fall Down	Robert Cormier
Are you in the house alone?	Richard Peck
Letters from the Inside	John Marsden
A Gathering Light	Jennifer Donnelly
Stone Cold	Robert Swindells

If you are interested in the problems facing young people

try these:

Key Stage 3

River Boy	Tim Bowler
The Secret Garden	Frances Hodgson Burnett
Tightrope	Gillian Cross
Goggle-eyes	Anne Fine
Up On Cloud Nine	Anne Fine

What Would Joey Do?	Jack Gantos
Happy	Keith Gray
Hoot	Carl Haasen
Red Sky in the Morning	Elizabeth Laird
Drama Queen	Chloe Rayburn
Feather Boy	Nicky Singer
The Illustrated Mum	Jacqueline Wilson

Key Stage 4

Massive	Gillian Bell
Junk	Melvin Burgess
Postcards from No Man's Land	Aidan Chambers
Dear Nobody	Berlie Doherty
Invisible Threads	Annie and Maria Dalton
Georgie	Malachy Doyle
The Lost Boys' Appreciation Society	Alan Gibbons
The Curious Incident of the Dog in the Night-time	Mark Haddon
Mates, Dates and Mad Mistakes	Cathy Hopkins
Underworld	Catherine MacPhail
The Shell House	Linda Newbury
The Other Side of Truth	Beverley Naidoo
Waiting for the Sky to Fall	Jacqueline Wilson
Last Seen Wearing Trainers	Jacqueline Wilson

If you like animal stories

try these:

The Christmas Rat	Avi
The Midnight Fox	Betsy Byars
My Family and Other Animals	Gerald Durrell
Jennie	Paul Gallico
Redwall series	Brian Jacques
Call of the Wild	Jack London
Out of the Ashes	Michael Morpurgo
Why the Whales Came	Michael Morpurgo
Not the End of the World	Geraldine McCaughrean

Mrs Frisby and the Rats of Nimh	Robert O'Brien
Silverwing	Kenneth Oppel
Magnus Powermouse	Dick King-Smith
Varjak Paw	S. F. Said

Useful website addresses mentioned in the text

Places to look for authors who visit schools
- www.booktrusted.co.uk/cbw/visit.html
- www.nawe.co.uk
- www.ncll.reading.ac.uk

www.seemore.mi.org/booklists/. This is probably the most comprehensive booklist I know. It covers books in any genre you could wish to find and even includes a 'If you liked this, try this' section.

www.scholastic.co.uk. Book fairs.

wendycooling@bookconsult.freeserve.co.uk. Wendy Cooling who has been a teacher, Head of the Children's Book Foundation and is now a freelance book consultant.

www.worldbookdayfestival.com/ is the World Book Day online. Here you can listen to the writers who are taking part in the Festival.

www.worldbookdayfestival.com/2004/. This website is worth a look even if it is not near the date because there are accessible archives of the previous Days with video clips of writers and teenagers talking about their appeal.

As it is World book Day there is a focus on Africa which can be accessed through www.bookaid.org.

Book reviews and suggestions
- *NATE News* is a source of reviews of teenage literature. You can access their website even if you aren't a member. New fiction is regularly reviewed at www.nate.org.uk.
- many newspapers review selections on a weekly basis, e.g.

the *Guardian* at www.books.guardian.co.uk/reviews/ or the *Independent* at www.enjoyment.independent.co.uk, then go to enjoyment→books→reviews.

- The Federation of Children's Book Groups also produces a series of booklists for students at different ages, e.g. Picture books, Books to Share, Confident Readers, Teenage Novels and Non-Fiction and Poetry books. Their website is at www.fcbg.org.uk.

www.listening-books.org.uk. Listening Books, also known as the National Listening Library, can help with suggestions for audio books.

www.the-zone.org.uk is the website of the Lincolnshire Library Service. This is a good website which includes Read Reviews, Review A Book, Information, Book Collections and Useful Links.

www.askchris.essexcc.gov.uk/adult/welcome.asp is the Essex Library service with suggestions for Inspirational reads.

The National Literacy Trust can be found at www.readon.org.uk/tbr.html. When you log on here go to the Secondary Schools Beyond the Big Read section and there are worksheets and a series of lessons related to the aims of the Literacy Strategy to help you to set up a balloon debate.

Author websites

- www.bbc.co.uk/arts/books/author/wilson/www.jkrowling.-com/
- www.mystworld.com/youngwriter/authors/jacqwilson.html

The home website for Young Writers at: www.mystworld.-com/youngwriter/index.html has a series of interviews which you could use as material for research. Here is a selection from that list:

- Michelle Magorian
- Gillian Cross
- David Almond
- Carol Ann Duffy
- Peter Dickinson
- Philip Pullman

- Kit Wright
- Michael Morpurgo
- Malorie Blackman
- Robert Swindells
- Anne Fine
- Brian Jacques
- Benjamin Zephaniah
- Terry Pratchett

www.lemonysnicket.com/
www.abhorsentrilogy.com/abhorsen.html
www.garthnix.co.uk
eidolon.net/homesite.html?author=garthnix
www.darrenshan.com/
www.homepage.eircom.net/~eoincolfer65/
www.kidsatrandomhouse.co.uk/jacquelinewilson/

Further list of useful websites on authors

Michael Morpurgo:	www.childrenslaureate.org/index.htm
Malorie Blackman:	www.malorieblackman.co.uk/pages/ games.html
Alan Gibbons:	www.alangibbons.com/
Anne Fine:	www.annefine.co.uk
Anthony Horowitz:	wwwchannel4.com/learning/microsites/B/ bookbox/authors/horowitz/index1.htm
Terry Pratchett:	www.turtlesalltheway.com/ (under construction at time of writing) www.terrypratchettbooks.com/
Louise Rennison:	www.teenreads.com/authors/au-rennison-louise.
David Almond:	www.davidalmond.com/
R. L. Stine:	www.scholastic.com/goosebumps/books/ stine/ www.thenightmareroom.com/

www.sharyn.org/authors.html. This website is an extensive collection of author websites. You should be able to find anyone you want here.

www.northamptonshire.gov.uk/Reading+Really+Matters/ Homepage.htm is also worth a look as it is another source of links to author websites.

The Carnegie website will support you in the shadowing scheme: www.carnegiegreenaway.org.uk/.

www.achuka.co.uk/ will give you a world of information on writers and books, as well as very useful links to other related sites. www.booktrust.org.uk/

Suggestions for teachers

www.englishonline.co.uk/ is one more website worth knowing about. Schools can buy into it with e-learning credits and gain access for whole departments and students. There are a number of goodies for teachers, including lesson plans and revision sessions for students on the most popular GCSE texts.

Typing 'writers@actis.co.uk' will take you to a section where writers challenge young people to develop an idea in relation to an extract from their own writing.

www.readerville.com is an American site dedicated to 'the social life of the mind', and if you haven't heard of www.bookcrossing. com try it.

www.4ureaders.net is a website for teenagers with book ideas and chatrooms.

www.word-of-mouth.org.uk.

The website www.myhomelibrary.org, endorsed by Anne Fine, is a website dedicated to encouraging young people to enjoy owning their own books.

Bibliography

Books

Meek, M. (1988) *How texts teach what children learn*. Woodchester, Glos.: The Thimble Press.

Styles, Morag, Bearne, Eve and Watson, Victor (eds) (1994) *The Prose and the Passion*. London: Cassell.

Styles, Morag and Drummond, Mary Jane (1993) *The Politics of Reading*, Cambridge: Homerton College/University of Cambridge

Laird, E. (2003) *The Garbage King*. Basingstoke: Macmillan.

Rees, C. (2003) *Pirates*. London: Bloomsbury.

McPhail, C. (2004) *Underworld*. London: Bloomsbury.

Updale, E. (2004) *Montmorency*. London: Scholastic.

Journals

Millard, Elaine and Marsh, Jackie, (2001) *Cambridge Journal of Education*, 31 (1): pp. 25–38. 'Sending Minnie the Minx Home: comics and reading choices'.

Burn, Andrew (2004) English, Drama, Media (June), *NATE*. 'From *The Tempest* to *Tomb-Raider*'.

Traves, P. (1988) 'Reading: the entitlement to be properly literate', *The English Magazine* 20 (Summer): 20–5.

Myhill, D. (2001) 'Why shaping and crafting matter', *The Secondary English Magazine* (October).

Index